WITHDRAWN

WITHDRAWN

HOME ENTERTAINING
AND ETIQUETTE

The Lenox Book of
HOME ENTERTAINING AND ETIQUETTE

by Elizabeth K. Lawrence

Crown Publishers, Inc., New York

Copyright © 1989 by Lenox, Incorporated

Published by Crown Publishers, Inc., 225 Park Avenue South,
New York, New York 10003

CROWN is a trademark of Crown Publishers, Inc.
LENOX is a trademark of Lenox, Incorporated
Manufactured in Japan

Library of Congress Cataloging-in-Publication Data
Lawrence, Elizabeth.
The Lenox book of home entertaining and etiquette.

Includes index.
1. Entertaining.   2. Table setting and decoration.
3. Etiquette.   I. Title.
TX731.L37   1989   642   88–18070
ISBN 0-517-57056-4

Design by Dana Sloan
10   9   8   7   6   5   4   3   2   1
First Edition

To Martha and Pope Lawrence,

who taught me how to enjoy

the company of friends

Contents

Foreword———————————————————————————viii

Introduction—————————————————————————x

Part One

THE GRACIOUS ART OF ENTERTAINING

1 The Perfect Party-Giver————————————————————3
2 Planning the Party——————————————————————9

Part Two

CELEBRATIONS

3 Weddings from Engagement to Reception————————————29
4 Celebrating Anniversaries and Birthdays——————————————49
5 Holiday Parties————————————————————————65
6 Casual Parties—————————————————————————87
7 Formal Occasions———————————————————————101

Part Three

TECHNIQUES OF TABLECRAFT

8 Setting the Table————————————————————————111
9 Choosing and Caring for Tableware—————————————————129
   Index————————————————————————————141

Foreword

Trenton, New Jersey, in the late 1800s fired the pottery of America and the dreams of Walter Scott Lenox. One hundred years ago in the flourishing center of American pottery, his creative instincts were directed toward the art of ceramics. Aware that the fledgling American industry was unable to produce a china fine enough to compete with centuries-old European ware, Walter Scott Lenox founded the Ceramic Art Company in 1889 determined to reverse the trend.

Acknowledgment that Walter Scott Lenox had succeeded—that America could produce china of the finest quality—came from President Woodrow Wilson. For the first time, an American china was selected for official White House use, a 1,700-piece Lenox dinnerware service. Since that time, the traditions of Lenox have become intertwined with the history of the White House, as subsequent services were commissioned by Presidents Franklin D. Roosevelt, Harry S. Truman, and Ronald Reagan.

Lenox takes great pride in superior craftsmanship. In 1965, having established the highest standards of excellence for china, Lenox acquired the oldest crystal glassblowing company in the country as the perfect complement to its fine china. With a proud heritage dating back to 1841, Lenox crystal is a leader in the art of handcrafted, full lead crystal. Lenox crystal has been selected for official use by the vice-president of the United States and by the State Department and Congress for presentation to dignitaries and heads of state throughout the world.

The same meticulous care and skill that go into the White House pieces are found in every piece of Lenox china and crystal. The assurance of excellence in craftsmanship, originality in design, and timeless beauty have made Lenox synonymous with the art of gracious living in America.

We approach our centennial with a sense of pride in the past and a commitment to the future. It is a fitting time to celebrate the art of entertaining. There's no better way than with *The Lenox Book of Home Entertaining and Etiquette* to help you make every occasion an expression of your personal taste. From a formal dinner to spur-of-the-moment gatherings to afternoon tea, it will guide you and inspire you.

Celebrate with us. Enjoy *The Lenox Book* for hours of good reading and years of wonderful entertaining.

James B. Chiles
President and Chief Operating Officer
Lenox, Incorporated

Introduction

Party-giving is an art, one born of the imaginative thinking of the people who give parties. Inspiration plays an important role in the best parties, providing the novel touches that make them perfect. But as with any art, party-giving is not mastered without lots of practice.

Almost without thinking about it, most of us begin to develop entertainment instincts long before our first official dinner party. In fact, the first celebrations many of us host are the tealess tea parties of early childhood or sleep-overs with best friends. Even if it's only a ten-minute party with lemonade and cookies, it is our party, born of our imaginations and planned solely by us.

More formal party-giving arrives with intermediate or high school. Dancing parties are often the chosen entertainments. The traditional formula features snacks and a constant diet of records. The secondary school years may also be the time to try out an adult-style dinner party, complete with a proper cooked meal. Surely by college the large group suppers cooked on a hot plate or a dorm kitchen range make their appearance.

By the time we reach adulthood, we may have more to our entertainment résumés than we realize. Even though so often we think of ourselves as completely untrained party-givers, the leap to serving dinner to the boss or arranging a supper party for ten is really only a small and logical step.

At the turn of the century things were different. Then a full dinner moved through successive courses of soup, fish, game, poultry, and meat, and offered dozens of vegetable dishes, before scaling down to an elaborate dessert or two, a cheese course, and closing with a savory. By those standards, most of all of us would feel untrained and unprepared without either the huge amounts of equipment or the household staff of the Victorian and Edwardian eras.

Perhaps it's some vestigial fear that causes many of us to panic when confronted with a true "adult" dinner party, one that really counts ("Oh, dear, no oyster forks —I can't serve a first course!"). It's true, of course, that few of us start out with complete sterling services for a dozen, including cream soup and bouillon soup spoons. But as we approach the twenty-first century, we can reflect on how different

things are today. Frankly, few of us routinely serve the sort of meals that begin with oysters on the half shell and soup and continue through numerous courses. Most often we see three-course meals. A first course, an entree, and dessert is a common combination; and even more frequently an entree, salad, and dessert compose the menu.

There is no denying that a certain romance surrounds our notions of the great entertainments of bygone eras or of the occasional lavish social and charity events that make appearances in the society columns. But for most mortals today's entertaining is much simpler on all fronts. Few people dress for dinner in evening gowns or white tie and tails except for the most formal occasions. Practically no one ever dresses formally at home—in fact, today dressing for dinner can mean changing out of white-collar work clothes and settling into blue jeans. For most people a really dressed up occasion calls for men in dinner jackets—in times past considered informal wear—and women in party dresses, long or short.

This book is intended for entertaining in our time. There are practical considerations that have changed our party habits—the time constraints of the two-career marriage is one significant one—yet there is a certain timelessness about stylish entertaining. This book aims to blend some of the great traditions of fine entertaining with modern lifestyles.

Most of us make the discovery several times in our lives: the most fun and rewarding of social experiences can be sharing food and drink with friends in one's own home. Thus, it is with home entertaining that this book is concerned. You don't have to have a grand house to entertain. You need not own the most expensive and elaborate china, crystal, and silver. You don't even need to be the world's best cook.

The key ingredients, in fact, are simply the wish to see your friends and a desire to have them enjoy themselves and one another. Armed with these—and the few fundamentals of organization contained in these pages—you can create a memorable party for your pleasure and that of your guests.

A Note on the Organization

This book is divided into three parts. Part One, "The Gracious Art of Entertaining," will tell you how to prepare for parties, and includes advice on how you can become the perfect host or hostess as well as specifics on the necessary planning stages. Included are discussions of how to create a guest list, the kind of invitations to choose (and when to use which kind), and how to go about hiring people and equipment for your party.

Part Two, "Celebrations," features a selection of parties. The twenty-eight parties are organized by theme (you'll find a baby shower in chapter 4, holiday parties in chapter 5, and a casual Sunday supper in chapter 6). The range is broad, and includes wedding parties, anniversaries and birthdays, family gatherings and holidays, parties with friends, dinner with the boss—even etiquette for dinner at the White House. They are intended to give you ideas and guidelines no matter what occasion you plan to celebrate.

When you're planning a party, find one of a similar size and theme in one of the chapters in Part Two. The anecdotes and the specific advice you'll find there are intended to help you anticipate the headaches and avoid the pitfalls of party-giving so that a good time can be had by all.

Part Three, "Techniques of Tablecraft," covers aspects of preparing your table for a party. The chapters in this section are full of detailed advice on organizing seating arrangements, setting the table beautifully, and choosing and caring for china, crystal, silver, and linens.

You will find in these pages the information you need to host your party (chapter 1) and to plan it for success (chapter 2). You'll find lots of ideas about kinds of parties and how to handle them (chapters 3 through 7), while you learn from the good fortune, as well as mistakes, of the innumerable party-givers whose experience provided the basis for this book. In chapter 8 you'll learn about the beautiful things that can adorn your table; in chapter 9 you'll learn how to choose and take care of them. So good luck with your entertaining and may your guests be forever charmed by your parties.

Part One

THE GRACIOUS ART OF ENTERTAINING

The Perfect Party-Giver

The desire to entertain friends comes first. Next follows the idea: the good hostess divines early on what sort of gathering would give her friends and herself pleasure. From then on it's merely a matter of making it happen to everyone's satisfaction.

As a hostess, you will develop what Dorothy Draper, one of the famous hostesses of the thirties and forties, called a flair for enjoyment. This flair is less a matter of transforming yourself than it is of designing your parties to suit your personality. If you feel most at home at formal parties, then get out your white damask; if you like informal ones, bring on the checked cloth. There are no rules that say you must give a certain kind of party, and the standards for giving a party must be yours, not someone else's. Since all parties revolve around the person giving them, you must be comfortable with your own.

In many ways the key to successful entertaining of any kind is in that ancient piece of Socratic wisdom, "To thine own self be true." If you don't like formal dinners using starched linens, elegant china, and the most brilliant of crystal, don't give them. On the other hand, if you like them but feel nervous about giving one, take courage, as they, like all parties, will be successful with planning and practice. Maybe you are more comfortable with casual pool parties, open houses, and potluck suppers. Perhaps you prefer dressy cocktail parties, romantic dinners for two, and breakfast in bed. Remember, the precise kind of party you favor doesn't matter; it's your attitude as a hostess or host that does.

If you entertain out of obligation, your guests will know it. On the other hand, if you are looking forward to the event, that attitude will be apparent to your guests. You can be nervous (everyone is), but if you start on a scale that feels comfortable and give a party that you would like to attend, chances are good that the pieces will fall together. And, equally important, your skills will develop.

Elegant desserts don't have to be rich and calorie-laden to judge from these poached pears.
CHINA: Orleans Blue CRYSTAL: Optika bowl; Optika floral vase

Parties can serve a multitude of purposes. Perhaps you want to rejoice in the coming of spring by inviting a few friends over for a dinner of spaghetti primavera, or maybe you want to toast your husband's new job with champagne and caviar. Such "purpose" parties are easy to understand—their reason for being is obvious. The guest list for such parties is usually obvious too, since they are geared for family and close friends.

Other parties have to serve specific purposes beyond the purely social or familial. Large gatherings such as open houses and cocktail parties provide an opportunity to bring together a larger circle of acquaintances, sometimes mixing business and social friends, but always with an eye for balance between the two. A dinner for office associates becomes both a social and business event, an opportunity to socialize within a formal context. Therefore, it is usually better to invite social friends to a different party. With a little thought the kind of party you want to give will be clear, and you can plan and prepare accordingly, so that your guests feel welcome and you feel comfortable.

The Warmest Welcome

There are certain techniques to develop that make guests realize from the moment they arrive that they're glad they came. Much of the success of a party depends on the cues you give, and the strongest among them is how you welcome your guests. The piecrust might burn and the salad might wilt, but your guests will hardly notice if they feel warmly welcomed.

There are a few simple methods for making guests feel welcome. The most important is your attitude—whether you are truly glad to see people. Easy, you say. Yes, but harried, unprepared hosts sometimes don't devote the required time and energy to their guests. The way to avoid such misfortune—which forces the guests themselves to make the party work—is to plan and prepare ahead.

In chapter 2 we will talk at length about guest lists and the importance of choosing guests who will enjoy one another. You need to plan food and drink that

---

You don't have to serve a dozen dishes when entertaining friends. Start with a stew or hearty soup that combines meat and vegetables, add a loaf of bread, a salad, and a little dessert, and you have a complete and generous meal. CHINA: *Chinastone Blue Brushstrokes* CRYSTAL: *Allure*

your guests will like and to prepare enough of the food in advance that you don't spend the whole evening in the kitchen. But there are other tricks, too.

Prepare your house for your parties: the first person who walks in shouldn't have to step over muddy shoes or children's toys. Instead the guests should know immediately that something special has been done for them. This does not mean you need to redecorate the house or spend a huge sum buying flowers. It does mean having the house ready when the first guest arrives. The house is neat and clean. Perhaps the fire in the grate is lit, certainly the table is set, and any special decorations are in place. Drinks are ready to be served and your guests made to feel as if they are really in the right place at the right time.

Having the house and food prepared are one thing. Having yourself prepared is another. People are embarrassed if the hostess or host is still dressing when they arrive. Most of us have been caught short on occasion. Haven't you? The first guest arrives and you're clutching a dust rag, having just finishing the vacuuming.

If at all possible, set aside for yourself a small block of time before people are scheduled to arrive. A few minutes will do. That's the time to put down your mixing spoon, brush the flour from your brow, and check everything over one last time. Look yourself over too, and take a few deep breaths. Allow yourself to anticipate the fun to come. Many people swear by a long bath and a fifteen-minute nap before guests arrive, both of which are lovely indulgences for the well-prepared party-giver.

Directing the Action

When the first guest arrives, you swing into action as the relaxed, perfect hostess. This does not mean, however, that you should sit back and let it all happen. For a typical at-home party, all guests should be greeted at the door by the hosts. As soon as coats are taken and the guests have had a chance to freshen up, if necessary, they should be offered something to drink. The host and hostess also should make introductions to the other guests, although this is not always possible in large groups. When introducing people, try to mention something about the person, such as what they do, or how you know them, or an interest you know they share with others.

During a party it is the duty of the host and hostess to make sure that new acquaintances or shy people are included in conversations. Sometimes this is done by way of introducing someone into a new group and bringing the conversation around

The Key Qualities of a
Good Party-Giver

■

1. *A sense of confidence, even showmanship.*
2. *An awareness of your own preferences. If you really like formal parties, give them. If you like casual ones, give those.*
3. *Thoughtfulness for guests' wishes and preferences.*

The Five Basic Rules for Entertaining

■

1. *Plan the party thoroughly so that you know what will need to be prepared and when.*

2. *Invite congenial guests who will enjoy one another.*

3. *Serve plenty of well-prepared food and beverages. Nothing shows you value your guests' comfort more than making sure you have plenty of everything.*

4. *Set an attractive table showing your china, crystal, silver, and linens to good advantage by taking care in their placement and using a little imagination.*

5. *Expect to have fun at your own party and your guests will do the same. Confidence breeds confidence.*

to a topic that everyone is able to participate in. More often than not, people will gather around you, thus making it easier for you to direct or redirect a conversation. One thing you must consciously avoid, however, is nervously dominating the conversation yourself, leaving others out. It's your party, but at the best parties everybody has a chance to shine.

It is also the hosts' duty to control the flow of the party. When it's time to serve dinner (usually about an hour after guests arrive for cocktails), you should lead the way. Tell people where to sit, alternating men and women, talkers and listeners. And don't hold up dinner too long waiting for one last guest. That's rude to the guests who arrived on time.

A thoughtful hostess and host are aware of their guests' needs and preferences. If you know that a favorite guest loves chocolate soufflé above all things, perhaps you will choose to serve a chocolate soufflé in the person's honor. Nancy Harmon Jenkins, writing in the *New York Times,* tells of the gracious hostess rewarding the guest who had admired the garden-fresh asparagus she served with a bundle wrapped in a clean napkin to be taken home. Not all of us have asparagus beds at our disposal, but paying attention to guests' preferences and taking note of them for the future just might win you encomiums as an outstanding hostess.

Finally, don't worry about disasters that could happen. They generally don't— and even if they do, people rarely notice them. If the mousse doesn't jell, serve it as pudding. If the ice cream was left out on the shelf and melted to a soup, mix it with fresh raspberries. Your guests will be charmed at your ingenuity. Remember, too, that mistakes are best left unannounced. If you forget to serve the salad, you should also forget to mention it. The conversation was so good that no one missed it anyway.

It's sometimes harder to be relaxed and gracious when entertaining for business. In fact, this is one of the most difficult kinds of entertaining, since there are so many factors involved. You need to seem professional, yet you are performing in a social setting; suddenly the world of the office has invaded your home. Yet in all kinds of entertaining, if you can plan and organize the party well, some of the anxiety that naturally occurs will dissipate.

In short, if the table is set, the food prepared, and the house in order, it is easier to relax and enjoy the company, whether the guests are the closest of friends or the most distant of acquaintances. Being the perfect party-giver is all about being relaxed and ready and being yourself.

Planning the Party

At its best, a party is a gathering of congenial people having fun. People arrive, they eat and drink, and, if the circumstances are right, have a merry old time. To borrow the words of the famous society hostess Elsa Maxwell, a party is "a sample case of the art of living together."

Most of us, however, don't think about parties in the abstract: we focus on what kind to give, whom to invite, and we anticipate a pleasant time. Parties are given to celebrate an occasion or to return the hospitality of friends or acquaintances; some allow business friends to get to know one another in a social context; others simply bring together compatible friends.

Whatever the impetus, the best parties seem effortless to the guests. The conversation sparkles, the food is good, and the setting is pleasing. We have all been to such gatherings and we all aspire to such success. But no matter how relaxed the host and hostess may have seemed at that ideal party, it isn't quite that simple.

The key is getting organized early; good planning is basic to the success of any party. The advance work doesn't have to be arduous, but it should be thorough. Take the example of a casual dinner party with a few friends.

A date is selected, the guests invited by phone. One way to prepare is to shop, clean up, and cook in a mad rush in the hours immediately before your guests arrive. The better way is to begin preparations a few days before the party. Plan the menu so that you can prepare a few things in advance—and actually do it. When the day of the party rolls around you make the rest of the preparations. The labor required when carried out in a considered, logical way seems natural, almost prescribed—and you don't end up a frazzled wreck as your guests arrive fresh and relaxed. Everyone will have a better time, especially you.

Although the entertaining most of us do is casual, circumstances can require that we give more elaborate

When a party has more than six or eight people, place cards are most helpful in directing guests to seats.

parties. Birthdays, weddings, anniversaries, holidays, and business dinners are obvious examples. In order to assure a seemingly effortless success at these out-of-the-ordinary events, good advance planning is even more important, and more elaborate, as such events may involve complicated logistics.

In preparing for any party, you need to have a fixed notion of what the party is about, who will be invited, what will be served, and how it is to be prepared and presented. But with bigger, fancier events, you need to think through the party even more thoroughly, preparing lists as you go. Will you need invitations? Do you need a site other than your home? How about entertainment, rental equipment, or kitchen or serving help?

As discussed in chapter 1, choosing the kind of party to give is one of the easiest parts of the planning process. Usually that decision almost makes itself. But whatever sort of party you're giving, your guests are more likely to feel like the welcome and congenial people you want them to be if you take care to address the key issues we will be discussing in the following pages. We'll cover everything from selecting your guests to preparing the food.

Creating a Guest List

If you have to think more than a minute or two about your guest list, spend a few more considering the subtle social aspects of the party. Before blithely rattling off names that come quickly to mind, think through the purpose and style of the party.

If it is a business-related dinner, you don't want to invite a couple of purely social friends, as they might well feel awkward. On the other hand, if the party is not intended to serve one specific purpose, balance the guests so that as many people as possible can participate in discussions, thus avoiding having too many work acquaintances talking office politics, leaving others out.

Inviting people you are just getting to know can help expand your circle of acquaintances, but you must make sure that they don't feel like outsiders. One way to do this is to be sure that the group is general enough that a few new people will fit in. Another way, particularly useful when a number of the other guests will have one thing in common, is to invite more than one newcomer or couple. But don't invite new friends to your dad's birthday party if all the other guests are to be family members.

Don't invite all strangers. Everyone might find things in common, have lively discussions, and go home fast friends, but they might just go home fast. Better to have some people whose conversational skills and personalities you know can fit easily into various situations and who thus help make the party flow smoothly. This lets newcomers find their own comfortable niches within groups and lessens your burden.

Since a good mix of people makes the most interesting party, try also to invite people from different generations. You will find that conversation is invariably more interesting when the views and perspectives of more than one age group are represented. Once you've gotten a mixture to your party, make sure they mix by seating people of different generations together.

Another issue to consider is the old-fashioned notion that you must have equal numbers of each sex. Most times it doesn't make sense to adhere to this doctrine, even at dinner parties. Try instead to anticipate which of your friends will like one another and how they will interact. That's more important than pairing them up evenly. Your single friends probably don't want to feel they've been fixed up anyway, particularly if the extra man or woman is not to their liking.

The bottom line is that you are creating a guest list in order to bring together people who are likely to have a good time with each other. Try to invite people whose interests are similar or whose personal styles will mesh. If you invite someone who is marvelous when surrounded by an appreciative group, then invite a couple of good listeners. Both the performer and the audience are likely to have a good time. Conversely, if you invite only performers, or only listeners, you might well have some strained conversations or deadening silences.

Once you have thought through who would be appropriate, sit down and make a tentative list of the people you would like to invite and the people you should invite. Then review the number with regard to your space and budget. If you need to trim, consider first who you really need to invite, then who you would really like to see. If there are any who don't fit either list, weed them out first. If you have early refusals, you can invite substitutes.

Finally, make up a list that you can refer to later on. In fact, if you're giving an elaborate party, it's often a good idea to make copies of the list. Use one for responses, one for the seating plan, and one for keeping a record of any gifts, should they be appropriate.

The Invitations

Invitations vary widely depending on the kind of party. They can be as simple as a telephone call on Sunday morning to ask close friends over for supper that evening. Decorated cards bought at a stationery store are appropriate for inviting people to a baby shower three weeks from tomorrow. You can create an invitation on a word processor—a word picture, for example, in the shape of a champagne glass to celebrate a friend's promotion. Then, of course, there is the formal wedding invitation, logical, highly structured, and engraved or calligraphed.

You will know pretty much the kind of invitation to use by the kind of party you give. However, there are a few useful guidelines to follow. We'll begin with the method we all use the most, the casual telephone call.

Inviting by Telephone

Telephoning is the simplest way to invite guests. You usually know before you hang up whether the person will come, and you can be sure he or she understands all of the information given.

The telephone invitation is also a good way to let someone know a little about the nature of the party. When you have people you want to bring together, you can say something like "We've talked about your meeting Rachel and Robert and we thought this would be a good opportunity." It's also a way for the guest to find out a little about the other guests. The person you are inviting may ask who else will be coming, but only after he or she has accepted or declined your invitation. (To ask before accepting is terribly bad manners, for it implies that the guest is interested in the party only if the guest list is satisfactory.)

Inviting by telephone is a good method if you are planning a casual event that does not involve too many people, but for more than a dozen the telephone approach can be confusing. It's hard to reach everyone by phone and get a response. Giving directions over the telephone is more difficult too, and often better handled with an enclosure to a written invitation.

The Written Invitation

Among the events that are best served by sending written invitations are anniversaries, birthdays, surprise parties, wedding and baby showers, formal occasions such as weddings, and, as we discussed, any party where the guest list is unwieldy. There

An Invitation to Tea

■

A written invitation to tea is similar to any formal invitation. It should be written on the face of fold-over notepaper in black or blue ink. Each line is centered. It should read this way:

In honor of Sarah Wyse
April 23
Tea at four o'clock
1920 South Street
New Haverford, Iowa

is a reason for this besides the time and trouble involved in telephoning many people: a written invitation shows that the party is important. Even when the gathering is only lighthearted fun like a costume or surprise party, a written invitation can convey something of its character as well as give a tangible reminder to the guest.

For all but the most formal of parties, the kind of invitation you send is entirely up to you. Many people like to send decorated preprinted invitation notes that all stationery stores carry. Other people like to create their own. The talented calligraphers among us can exercise their skills, but even for those of us who lack pretty penmanship, wonders can be done with a rubber stamp and copying machine. Creating your own invitation to suit a party can be an added pleasure.

If you have no desire to exercise your graphic vision, use commercially available invitations. If you find them too pat or familiar, use simple note cards. In many ways the most intimate invitation is a note saying something like "John and I would like very much for you to come to dinner January 26th at 8:00 P.M. We'll be an informal

Invitations are available in all sizes and a wide variety of styles, from extremely informal, even whimsical, to the most formal.

group of eight. Please let us know if you can join us. Hope to see you then." Some people who entertain a great deal have their own invitation cards printed with their names and a standard phrase such as "Mr. and Mrs. John Jones request the pleasure of your company" followed by blanks for the appropriate information.

Formal Invitations

These days formal invitations are used most often for weddings, but occasionally for other events, particularly business meals, dances, and debuts.

Correct invitations are printed on white or cream stationery, usually with black ink in an elegant, conservative type style. The design should be simple and unadorned. Everything is spelled out, including street and state names. When the time of day is on the half hour, it is written "half after one" or "half past one o'clock." "One thirty" is not used. The wording throughout is prescribed and simple.

A proper wedding invitation reads this way:

> *Mr. and Mrs. John Aston Smith*
> *request the honor of your presence*
> *at the marriage of their daughter*
> *Anna Louise*
> *to*
> *Mr. Eustis Williams McBride*
> *on Saturday, the twenty-second of May*
> *nineteen hundred and ninety-two*
> *at two o'clock*
> *Saint-Martin-in-the-Fields,*
> *Fifty-one Marblehead Lane*
> *Westminster, Massachusetts*
> *and afterward at*
> *The Women's Club*
> *Sixteen Hundred Wisconsin Avenue*

The message of this invitation is very simple: the guest learns who is giving the party, who is getting married to whom, and where and when. A formal invitation should be sent four to eight weeks in advance of the party and may include a request that the guest respond by a specified date.

These days everything seems more complicated than in times past, and you certainly see it in wedding invitations. Often the parents of the couple are divorced and thus several names will appear. To whom do I respond, you ask? Respond to the first name on the invitation and mail it to the address found on the envelope, unless a response address is specified on the invitation.

An invitation to any event should be as straightforward as possible. Whether it's a telephone call, a clever cut-paper sculpture, a preprinted invitation with Miss Piggy on it, or the most austere engraved invitation on expensive rag stock, state clearly the purpose of the party, the date, time, and place. Occasionally you may also want to state the dress preference (for a pool party: "Bring your bathing suit") or refer to presents (for a twenty-fifth wedding anniversary: "Your presence alone is the best you can bring").

The only abbreviations used in a formal invitation are Mr., Ms., Miss, Mrs., Dr., and r.s.v.p. or R.S.V.P. ("*Répondez, s'il vous plaît*," which literally translates as "Respond, if you please" but implies, "Please let us know if you are coming"). The other correct response requests include "The favor of a reply is requested" and "Please reply to."

In recent years more people have taken to enclosing response cards, particularly with formal invitations. That way they can be sure of the number of people attending, because so many people, when confronted with having to compose a response, will put it off. This is a particular problem when caterers are used, for they must know the exact count well in advance of an event. In days gone by, no one would have dreamed that their guests would need such a card, as any thoughtful person would have written their reply. Today, however, many people often don't respond unless provided with a self-addressed envelope and card.

Not everyone in the world uses response cards, nor do you need to use them when included, and it is really quite easy to compose a formal reply. As with the invitation, the wording is prescribed and very simple. The reply must tell the hostess that you understand who is giving the party, the date, and whether you will be attending; the form is basically the same for an acceptance or regret. A correct reply goes like this:

Mr. and Mrs. James Arlen Jones
accept with pleasure
the kind invitation of
Mr. and Mrs. John Aston Smith
for Saturday, the twenty-second of May

If you enjoy writing replies you may be a little more elaborate and write:

Mr. and Mrs. James Arlen Jones
accept with pleasure
the kind invitation of
Mr. and Mrs. John Aston Smith
to the marriage of their daughter
Anna Louise
to
Mr. Eustis Williams McBride
on Saturday, the twenty-second of May
at two o'clock
at Saint-Martin-in-the-Fields
and afterward at
The Women's Club
Sixteen Hundred Wisconsin Avenue

All formal replies should be written on white or cream stationery, using a black or blue pen. The wording should be centered. You will also notice that periods are not included at the ends of the sentences.

Being able to respond to an invitation immediately is the ideal, but this isn't always possible, particularly when coordinating schedules with a spouse or family members. When you are the recipient of an invitation of any kind, treat it as important: even if it isn't a major event to you, it is to the party-giver. Respond as soon as possible in order not to hold up the planning.

When accepting an informal invitation, it makes the hostess feel good if you express enthusiasm or interest. When refusing an invitation, give a brief explanation of why you cannot attend. Responding with a curt yes or no can make the host or hostess feel that you regard the party as an unwanted obligation, whether you attend or not.

The Perfect Party—at Home?

The sets aren't as important as the actors, of course, but it's a rare play that doesn't benefit from appropriate and appealing staging. In the same way, any party —from a buffet supper to an evening ball—benefits from special attention to its setting. Indeed, for many people the setting is crucial to the celebration.

You may wish to rent the fanciest hall in town, but keep in mind that the location doesn't have to be the most exotic or romantic or palatial. For many people home is the site of choice for all kinds of parties, and you don't have to have the perfect house to give the perfect party. If you're lucky enough, however, to have a beautiful house with lots of space and well-kept grounds, you can probably accommodate any party, whether it's a formal dinner for 20 or a wedding for 150. If you have a pool or tennis court, the options are even greater.

Weddings, of course, offer many possibilities for creative entertaining. Take the wedding of a couple who were married in the rose garden of an arboretum. The wedding was small and the ceremony was held amid extravagant beds of roses and boxwood hedges. The bride and groom, minister, maid of honor, and best man walked into the center of the mazelike garden. The ceremony that followed was simple, the music provided by a pair of folk singers with lilting harmonies. After the ceremony everyone greeted the couple and formal photos were taken of the bride and groom, family, and guests in the beautiful garden. Then everyone meandered back to the bride's parents' house, where a reception was held. The settings—the arboretum for the ceremony and the family yard for the party—were a happy combination of the elegant formal garden and the casual warmth of the family's home.

Another couple thought they would have their wedding and reception in a hotel or club. They looked at possible sites for months and found nothing within their budget that seemed just right. As a last resort, they looked carefully at their apartment. With a little imaginative thinking and preparation they were able to transform it into the perfect site for a winter wedding. They moved most of the furniture into the extra bedroom and filled the apartment with flowers. It was a little cramped, but on that brisk winter day no one noticed. So even if your instinct is to go elsewhere, home may be your best bet.

Hiring the Help and Rental Equipment

When planning a party for more than twenty people, you'll probably want to consider hiring people to help. You may also need to rent equipment (even if you have enough china and crystal for thirty people, chances are good you don't have enough chairs to seat them for dinner). The outside help may be necessary not only to help with those extra chairs, but also with passing cocktail foods, tending bar, and the more basic tasks, such as cleaning the house and yard and minding the children.

To begin with, use the sources you have. If you have someone who comes in to clean, ask if you can hire her to help get the house ready for a party and to help clean up afterward. If you need more than one person, ask if she has a friend you could hire. If you don't have such a resource, you can go through a temporary help agency or ask friends who have hired party help before.

Ask a regular baby-sitter for extra time for the party. You might need it as you get ready for the event as well as during the party. If guests are welcome to bring their children—who can then make it one big playtime—you'll probably want to hire a sitter or two to supervise the little guests.

Next come the slightly harder decisions that may go beyond your normal purview: hiring a caterer, waiters, waitresses, bartenders, and pantry help. For many people, finding the right caterer is the key element for a successful party. But what distinguishes the right caterer from the wrong one? That's the easy part. You want to hire the one who makes you comfortable and whose food and style you like.

How do you find this perfect caterer? First, think of the most successful catered parties you've attended and who did the food. Then ask the friend who hired the caterer for the name and phone number. You can also ask friends to recommend caterers they have liked. Or perhaps you've seen articles in the newspaper on local caterers.

Once you have some names, call them, explain the party you will be giving, the kind of food you would like to have, and your budget. A good caterer will tell you right off if it's the kind of party he or she does and if they can work within your financial constraints. You should know by the conversation with each caterer whether you want to carry the discussion any further. If you do, make an appointment to meet. At the meeting you will discuss the menu and budget more fully. If your party is to be held during a holiday or a particularly busy season, plan to book your caterer well in advance, or you may be disappointed.

When it comes to hiring serving people and kitchen help, there are several methods. First, if you are using a caterer, he or she usually has a regular group of people to call upon. This is one of the advantages of a caterer, for it is usually his or her responsibility to handle the details of hiring people and arranging for rentals, in addition to providing the food and cleaning up afterward.

If you don't plan to work with a caterer but need help, you might want to start again with asking friends who they have used satisfactorily. If that doesn't work, try contacting a local culinary school, college placement bureau, club, caterer, or temporary help agency. Whoever you use, from a high school student to a professional who works through an agency, you will want to make sure that the person is capable and honest. Ask for references and then, if you feel it necessary, meet with them.

Hiring Rentals

Say you need a marquee, a dance floor, or fifty palm trees. How do you go about finding the extra equipment? You call rental companies and hire it.

Almost everything you can imagine can be rented, from nickelodeons to wedding clothes to everything in between. First, determine what you will need, then turn to the local Yellow Pages for its rental company listings. Some companies specialize in certain kinds of equipment, such as tents and dance floors or cooking equipment. Some are full service and handle everything. Pick several that sound appealing, then call to determine the costs and availability of the goods you need.

Look for a company that has a wide selection of merchandise and whose staff seems professional and helpful. A good rental company will have not only twelve dozen highball glasses, but several varieties at several prices, depending on the quality. Make sure they understand that you want to know the range. Also be sure to ask how long a lead time the company needs, how they deliver, and what their payment policy is.

When you speak with a rental company, make sure you get not only a phone quotation but a written one, too. In fact, ask if they have a catalog, price list, or other literature you can use for reference. Once you have quotes in hand, compare them, call back, and place an order when you have your date and needs decided.

Organizing Entertainment

Different parties have different musical needs. A tea or reception might call for a string quartet, a cocktail party for a pianist with a vocalist, a coming-of-age party for a rock group or disc jockey with turntable.

Discovering the kind of music you need is simple; finding it takes a little more work. Every major city has its Lester Lanin—a band that is the sine qua non of big wedding and party music. This is the full-scale band that plays at society functions as well as the parties of just plain folks. These bands are usually expensive and booked well in advance, so make your reservations early.

Whatever your needs, chances are it's out there: musical groups abound, so, as usual, it's largely a matter of finding them. One place to start is the Yellow Pages under "Musicians." Check the listings, choose a few that look appropriate, and give a call. With a brief conversation you can determine the kind of music, the price, and the group's availability. When you find a suitably priced band, it's a good idea to arrange to see and hear them, if only briefly. Find out where they are playing next, and stop in for a few minutes.

Other methods for finding good music include getting in touch with the music department of a local college and asking for recommendations or contacting the musical director of a local orchestra, community musical group, or church for suggestions. These are often great sources for less professional but quite talented (and usually less costly) groups.

Although a group may be the most immediate form of musical entertainment, an evening of music coordinated and managed by a disc jockey can be a good alternative to hiring a live act. The advantages include having both the original versions of favorite songs and the newest of the new. And, of course, it usually costs less to hire a record spinner than it does to hire a group of musicians, especially if union wages are the norm in your vicinity. Disc jockeys can often be hired through local radio stations, by word of mouth, through a local college radio station, or even through a community bulletin board ad or newspaper advertisement. Again, interview the candidates and ask for a sample of their work. They'll probably have tapes you can borrow. Check their references before hiring as well.

Music is not your only entertainment choice. Clowns at children's birthday parties are particularly popular, as are magicians, most of whom advertise in local newspapers or in the Yellow Pages under "Entertainers."

Holiday parties often have entertainment, too. Santa Claus is always popular, as are the Easter Bunny and Father Time. Character actors are usually hired for such parts. One method for finding such actors is to call the special events department of a local department store or mall. Another is to call a talent agency.

There are certain ground rules for hiring people to entertain that save unnecessary misunderstandings. In the first place, all rates must be clearly understood. Second, the length of the entertainment must be determined. In the case of musicians playing at a party that might last later than anticipated, it's a good idea to establish whether the band is willing to stay on later, too, and if so, how long and for how

Meal Courses

■

The Formal Dinner

1. *First course (soup, fruit, or shellfish)*
2. *Fish course (never served if shellfish is the first course or fish the entree)*
3. *Entree (includes vegetables)*
4. *Salad*
5. *Dessert*

The Informal Dinner

1. *First course (soup, fruit, or shellfish), optional*
2. *Entree (includes vegetables)*
3. *Salad, optional*
4. *Dessert*

Luncheon

1. *First course, optional*
2. *Entree (includes vegetables)*
3. *Dessert*

much more money. In all cases determine whether you need to provide any special equipment, such as a piano, sound equipment, or lighting. Ask for the names of suppliers and then get quotes. Factor these extra costs into your budget.

Planning the Menu

Every party has a menu, even if only cocktails and cheese are served. If such simple fare is all you require, you don't really need to worry much about preparation and timing of dishes, or whether each course balances with its predecessor and successor, or whether your kitchen is suitable for preparing a meal. Your problems are confined to determining what kinds of cheese and what sorts of crackers to serve with your cocktails.

However simple or complex the food and drink at your party, you must plan your meal so that it suits the flow of the event. Accomplishing this lies at the heart of entertaining.

Balance is the key element in menu planning. At its most basic, a lunch or dinner menu is composed of elements from the four basic food groups: meat, poultry, fish, or other protein; vegetable or fruit; bread or cereal; milk or other dairy products. Most people instinctively include a representation of each of the groups at a meal, providing their guests with a properly balanced meal.

Balance is also about more subjective concerns, such as complementary flavors, textures, and colors served in such a way that the combinations are appealing and appropriate. Meals that consist of too many similar elements tend to be boring. Duck with orange sauce served with winter squash and a salad with honey dressing has too many sweet flavors. A veal stew served with cauliflower and rice is too bland in color. A cheese soufflé served with pureed vegetables and a pudding for dessert has no variation in texture. A little diversity in the menu planning will help make your party memorable.

Think back to the food of the most successful parties you have given or attended. Was the combination of flavors and aromas pleasing? Were sweet dishes balanced with savory? Were crisp and chewy textures set off by smooth and creamy ones? Was there a variety of color on the assembled plates? Did the courses flow smoothly from the appetizer through the main course to the dessert? Was the soup hot and the ice cream slightly soft? There may not have been many meals in which all of these things worked smoothly, but the goal of planning a menu carefully is to achieve perfect balance and timing.

Timing is a purely personal matter and depends largely on your own work methods. Many people find that preparing a meal in stages and as much in advance as possible works best. Others like to spend a concentrated day in the kitchen. It is safe to say, though, that if you are a busy person trying to sandwich party-giving between work and family obligations, you will probably find it easier to prepare some things in advance and not rely on dishes that take a great deal of last-minute preparation. Leave the soufflés for thirty to chefs and caterers whose sole job is to work in the kitchen. As a hostess or host your duties are ample without assuming greater burdens than necessary.

Keep in mind what can be done well in advance and what needs to be done just before serving. Stews and soups can and usually should be made a day or two in advance. Any foods that must be marinated naturally benefit from advance preparation. Desserts such as charlottes, puddings, and some cakes can be made a day or two ahead, too. Roasts and baked dished can be prepared a few hours in advance and be cooking when guests arrive. Most salad dressings should be made early to allow the flavors to mingle. Salad greens and vegetables can be washed and dried up to a day in advance and cut or torn an hour or two before serving.

Try to discover what can be done ahead by studying your proposed recipes and by making scheduling notes. Record what must sit out for an hour before serving and how long a certain sauce needs to simmer. Then you can make lists of the various tasks that will form the basis of a work plan.

Another wise rule to follow when cooking for guests is: stick to dishes that you know. How do you learn new party dishes if all you ever serve are your standards? Or what if you are just starting out and do not have much experience? Interesting problems, particularly since many of us just don't have the time to try out a number of dishes well in advance. For some party-givers entertaining is the arena in which they perfect new dishes. Try to limit those experiments to good friends. If you yearn to try something a little risky, try to make it in advance to test it. Choose test recipes carefully by reading them several times over and imagine just how you would go about making the dish. Sometimes the imaginative process will show you that a dish is impractical for a party.

The other helpful method in menu planning is to follow the suggestion of Christopher Idone, co-founder of the famous caterers Glorious Food. He advises

An assembled bar complete with lowball and highball glasses. CHINA: *Eclipse* CRYSTAL: *Windswept*

The Fully Stocked Bar to Serve 25

■

Alcohol

SUMMER	WINTER
1 quart Scotch	*3 quarts Scotch*
1 quart bourbon	*2 quarts bourbon*
3 quarts vodka	*2 quarts vodka*
3 quarts gin	*2 quarts gin*
2 quarts rum	*1 quart rum*
4 bottles dry white wine or champagne	*4 bottles dry white wine or champagne*
2 bottles dry red wine	*2 bottles dry red wine*
1 dozen bottles wine cooler	*6 bottles wine cooler*
1 dozen bottles beer	*1 dozen bottles beer*

If the crowd is particularly young, increase the amount of vodka, rum, and beer and decrease the amount of Scotch, bourbon, and gin. If the crowd is health-conscious, increase the amount of wine and decrease the amount of liquor.

Allow 1 pound of ice per person plus 10 pounds for every 25 people.

Mixers

SUMMER	WINTER
10 quarts tonic water	*5 quarts tonic water*
6 quarts club soda (10 if serving white wine spritzers)	*10 quarts club soda*
2 quarts ginger ale	*2 quarts ginger ale*
3 quarts cola	*2 quarts cola*
4 quarts diet soda	*3 quarts diet soda*
5 limes	*3 limes*
5 lemons	*3 lemons*

AT ALL TIMES

1 small bottle dry vermouth if martinis will be served

Ice bucket, water pitcher, shot glass, paring knife, bottle opener, corkscrew

limiting yourself to one "bravura course" and not to try to outdo yourself on each one. That way the rest of the meal can be constructed around the special course rather than compete with the others. Naturally you want each course to be special and taste and look wonderful, but keep most of them simple.

Another thing to consider when planning a menu is the tastes of your guests. Once you know who will be coming, it's a good idea to sit down and examine the guest list for possible preferences or aversions. It is truly gratifying when you serve something that your guests obviously relish, but, conversely, there are few things more embarrassing than serving a special course and suddenly remembering that one of your guests is allergic to shellfish or doesn't like lamb or some other key ingredient.

When giving a very large party, you cannot be expected to anticipate the needs and preferences of all your guests. Yet it is wise to stick to familiar dishes or ingredients that are widely appreciated—keep the brains and sweetbreads for the known adventurers at a more intimate gathering. You don't have to serve bland or uninteresting dishes, but be aware that dishes with unusual ingredients often require a sophisticated palate to be appreciated. Keep in mind that older people often prefer less spicy food than younger ones. They also tend to eat more rounded meals than young people, who increasingly make dinners of appetizers and single courses.

Advance preparation frees up the host or hostess to enjoy the company of guests. Here a hearty stew and baked apples are ready and waiting. CHINA: *Chinastone Blue Pinstripe rectangular baker*

A postwedding party at home featuring simple food—cold sliced roast beef, roasted peppers, cold pasta salad, and mozzarella with sliced tomatoes and sautéed spinach—can be the most relaxed gathering of all the wedding parties. CHINA: *Monroe*

Preparing the Food

Unless you have unlimited time and help, cooking for a party needs to be done efficiently. You shouldn't have to spend the entire evening in the kitchen, offering your guests barely a smile and a hello. That's not fun for you or them, as you are too important to the overall party to be siphoned off to the back of the house. There are a number of ways of organizing the meal to suit the time allowable, from doing everything yourself in advance to involving your guests. Whatever method you choose, it should be planned.

Once you have created a menu, it's time to create a menu work plan. Such a plan sets out each of the tasks to be performed in sequence so that you don't have to rely on memory to juggle the many details that may weigh heavily as the party approaches.

Gather your recipes together and read through each one, noting when the various steps need to be performed. Then coordinate the tasks. Begin by listing every major preparation beginning about a week before the party for an elaborate event, a day or

so for simpler ones, ending with the tasks to be performed the day of the party, right up to the moment of serving.

Such lists should take special account of one of the most crucial elements of preparation—the timing. The worst fear of many cooks is not having dishes ready for the table at the appropriate time. Hot dishes must be hot, cold dishes cold, and the pilaf ready when the lamb chops are done. If you cook a lot, timing becomes second nature, but when the party starts your systems are likely to be disrupted. That is when your list of tasks can save the day. Your list will help you remain organized and keep your confidence from flagging.

When you actually get ready to cook, approach it systematically. Do what professional chefs do and set out every piece of equipment and every ingredient you will need for a dish before you begin to cook. Few of us do this regularly, since we often feel rushed to get things under way, but it really adds to the efficiency of preparation. How many times have you found yourself engaged in conversation with a guest while trying to finish a dish and discovered that you'd lost your place because you didn't have everything you needed measured and ready to go? Faithfully set out and measure every ingredient of a dish and line them up in sequence. That way, nothing can be left out.

The Final Think-through

The old cliché tells us that there is no substitute for experience. And it's true. That doesn't mean you shouldn't dare to take on what you've never done before; what it suggests is that serving an engagement party buffet for forty is good practice for serving the starving two hundred at your daughter's wedding.

You're on your own now. Be confident—steeling yourself for the odd unexpected turn, but believing it will work is no small part of making it work. There is one little trick that works.

At least a day or two in advance of the event, find yourself a quiet place and a few uninterrupted minutes. Sit down with your work plan and walk yourself mentally through each step. You may even want to physically walk from food preparation to serving areas. Consider who will be doing what and when. Don't leave out the drink mixing and the coat taking or anything else—everything takes time and consideration.

Now you are ready for the party. For ideas and inspiration, read on.

Part Two

CELEBRATIONS

Weddings from Engagement to Reception

Weddings are universal symbols of happiness. They represent both the excitement of the present and the great promise of the future. There's an energy to weddings and it's contagious to anyone who comes near. Even the peripheral parties happen on a more excited level, as people want to give and share in the events.

Weddings are the most romantic and fulfilling of all parties, and our images of them begin in childhood. Almost everyone remembers the first wedding he or she attended and the sense of magic it conveyed. For some people the recollection is of a bride in a wide hoop skirt and a haze of tulle. Your first memory may be of watching your best friend as a flower girl, throwing delicate rose petals in the bride's path as she walked up the aisle. The scene held your complete attention, as did champagne bubbling in the fountain, flowing from tier to tier, at the reception afterward.

Weddings often are made up of a number of events. The first is often an engagement party given by the parents or friends of the bride and groom. (There may be more than one engagement party, if, for example, the bride and groom come from different parts of the country.) Bridal showers for both women and men often take place a few short weeks before the wedding. Tradition once required that the groom give a dinner for his attendants at which the bride was toasted, but that has largely been supplanted by bachelor parties, given by male friends of the groom.

The fêtes lead right up to the wedding. On the evening before, the rehearsal dinner is usually given for the bridal party and close relatives by the groom's family. As a counterpart to the groom's dinner, the bride may host a lunch for her attendants just before the wedding. But the pièce de résistance is, of course, the reception and often a more informal postwedding party at home.

Wedding parties are forever interesting because of their diversity. One can be a formal seated dinner, another a pool party, a third a casual dinner at a quiet restaurant.

This quiet haven is the bride's dressing room, complete with the key elements of her attire.

And no matter what they are like, almost everyone is primed for a good time. With that thought in mind, let's begin with the engagement party.

The Engagement Party

Engagement parties can be the most relaxed of the parties preceding a wedding. Given primarily to introduce the soon-to-be family member to friends and relatives, they range from rather formal affairs to spontaneous celebrations. Almost anything goes.

Some couples choose to give a party apparently for the sake of having a party, only to announce their marriage plans during the evening. Sometimes friends or family give a party in honor of a couple. Engagement parties can be given anytime before a wedding, but usually before the heavy planning gets under way and before the showers and other wedding parties are held.

For people who prefer intimate parties with close friends, the nicest engagement party can be a dinner with the people you plan to ask as attendants. Often a romantic or cozy dinner seems a particularly good time to announce such a special event. It's often enhanced by a bottle of champagne that's chilled, awaiting the declaration.

At the other end of the spectrum, large cocktail parties are often given by the bride or groom's family. These parties allow the relatives and friends of the family to meet the newcomer before the wedding. These parties are given frequently in private clubs or at home by socially active families.

One couple hosted an inspired engagement party for some dear friends. It was a buffet dinner for the couple's families, a chance to meet outside the milieu of either family's home. The food, which was quite simple, was picked up from a caterer on the day of the party. The hosts provided the drinks, music, and space. The party site —their apartment—provided an automatic focus of conversation, for it was in mid-renovation. Roughly plastered walls and plywood counters and floors greeted the guests, who gasped slightly but soon felt part of a work-in-progress (not that they were put to work). Simple arrangements of flowers contrasted nicely with the rough condition of the apartment, providing the only decoration. The dining table was bare, but set with pretty serving pieces and the couple's most attractive casual china. The overall effect was certainly casual and quite inviting.

The party was a great hit for the food was good, the setting unusual, the participants happy, and the talk animated. The only hitch came over dessert. The mother of the bride had volunteered to bring a special Italian cake and had forgotten it. The guests ate doughnuts and ice cream instead and laughed about it later.

There's no single correct way to handle the announcement. The couple may have already gone public in advance of a party, either informally or in the newspaper. In that case, the invitation can make the purpose of the party explicit, reading something on the order of "Jim and I so hope you can come for dinner on January 29th in honor of our daughter Mary and John Jones." Some people try to keep the news a secret until the party—if the bride's parents are giving the party, the news is often broken by the father of the bride, who makes a toast to the couple.

What better way to convey the good wishes of assembled friends and family than with a toast?
CRYSTAL: *Monroe*

If it is to be a surprise announcement, you shouldn't be surprised yourself if word has already gotten out. Good news travels fast, and at a large party people often guess what's up when they see the bride-to-be, her mother, and the groom-to-be receiving people. For some people announcing their engagement is an opportunity to do something dramatic, silly, or just fun. It can be as simple as having the couple's names printed on balloons that fill the house or as elaborate as having a skywriter spell out the news above a lawn party. Sometimes singing telegrams serenade the party or a musician will begin playing the couple's song as a prelude to an announcement.

An engagement party is a good opportunity for a little inventiveness. The party itself, the setting, the food, and even the news of the engagement all lend themselves to an imaginative approach.

The Bridal Shower

A shower is one of the traditional parties for the bride leading up to the wedding. In these more enlightened times co-ed bridal showers are on the increase, but most often they remain an all-women's preserve.

Usually given on a weekend afternoon or weekday evening, such events are a chance to shower the bride with small useful gifts for the house or personal items. Sets of dish towels, eggbeaters, a coffeepot, a nightgown, or pretty scarf are common shower gifts. Sometimes a theme is specified, suggesting that kitchen, bath, household goods, or lingerie be given. When men are included, wine and accompanying paraphernalia are often given.

Bridal showers have their own sets of customs. Showers are generally given by good friends or members of the wedding, not close family members (parents and siblings), for the simple reason that for the immediate family to give a shower appears to be asking for gifts.

The party itself has customs, too. In some parts of the country a corsage is made for the bride and a specially decorated cake is common. Party games are usual, too, including one in which the person who keeps a record of the gifts given makes up a

---

Bridal showers have become almost as much a tradition as the wedding itself, whether you serve champagne and exquisite desserts like these or iced tea and salad at poolside. CHINA: *Symphony platter and bowl; Charleston tray* CRYSTAL: *Classic Laurel*

story using each of the items. It often goes something like: "John [the groom] walked out of the bedroom only to see Mary [the bride] wearing a frying pan [first item on the list.]" It can be quite silly or genuinely hilarious, depending on the skills of the storyteller. Another of the customs is for someone to save all the bows on the packages and attach them to a paper plate, so that at the end of the party a bouquet has been created that the bride uses as a stand-in at the rehearsal.

Office showers for both men and women are some of the most inventive, since co-workers often don't know the intended or what the couple really needs. One idea for an office shower is to have someone dummy up an invitation in the style of a formal wedding invitation and send copies to co-workers. In the bottom left-hand corner you might include a small elegant postscript reading, "$3.00 limit." This makes for highly inventive (if mostly useless) gifts that are within the range of everyone at the company. No one person's present stands out as more expensive or more thoughtful than another's. In fact, the purpose of a shower present is to serve as a memento rather than to compete with a wedding present.

Sometimes, however, people get carried away at showers. When a couple is given a television or a VCR as a shower present, all other gifts pale in comparison, leaving all but the overgenerous feeling they have somehow let people down with their modest presents. If you plan to give an elaborate present, save it for the wedding or give it privately.

Showers given for the bride and groom jointly are a chance for people to show some creativity and are a particularly good way of including the groom, who often gets a great deal less attention than his bride. They are a chance for people to get together and share the warm feelings of the wedding as much as possible. Such showers, increasingly popular, are often given on weekends, either during the day or evening, and often take the form of a cocktail or dinner party. People give presents to the couple rather than to just the bride.

Sometimes the bride and groom are given more than one shower. It helps greatly if the guest lists have been coordinated so that the same people aren't invited to more than one; they feel they have to bring additional gifts, which is an unfair burden. Ask the bride's mother or the maid of honor for a gift suggestion if the shower is to be a surprise; otherwise, ask the bride.

These days showers can be cocktail parties, buffets, afternoon teas, Sunday lunches, pool or garden parties. They can be cake-and-punch parties, with the food served on beautiful china and white linen, or supper with the most casual of china and glass. They can feature caviar and crudités with a glass of champagne or hot

Shower Etiquette

■

The Guest

Bring your gift in person. Shower gifts are not sent from a store, as these parties are informal and personal.

The present should be gift-wrapped in appropriate all-purpose or shower paper. Bright paper and ribbons make colorful packages that stand out; pastels and other soft shades make demure statements.

A card or tag must be attached to avoid confusion. There is nothing more embarrassing for the bride and groom than finding out when the dust settles that they don't know who gave certain gifts.

When presents are opened, oohs and aahs and nice words about every gift are the rule—for the guests as well as the bride and groom.

You must also remember that all attention should focus on the featured players, the bride and the groom.

The Bride or Groom

If you are the recipient of a shower, you, too, have responsibilities. The first is to have a good time, of course, and be grateful for the kind attention and thoughtfulness of your friends, even if you hate surprise parties.

You should also personally thank each person who came and brought a gift. You should then also thank them in writing. Anyone who sent a present but could not attend should be thanked in writing. This will be good practice for all the thank-you notes you must write for wedding gifts.

dogs and hamburgers grilled to perfection over an open pit of glowing charcoal.

Suit the party to the bride and groom. If they are athletic, consider giving an active party. A weekend afternoon may lend itself to some sort of physical activity that can include both men and women, such as softball, volleyball, or swimming. If the couple is shy and retiring, a quiet party such as a small dinner is probably more appropriate than a large and rambunctious cocktail party.

People love to give a surprise bridal shower, but it requires a little extra planning. First, it must be held far enough in advance that the bride is not likely to be suffering last-minute anxiety over organization and thus be distracted or unable to enjoy herself. But it must be held close enough to the wedding that the couple's needs have been established. Also, make sure that whatever ruse is devised to bring a woman to her shower (or a couple to theirs) that it allows her (them) to be dressed appropriately. This is a common courtesy and will avoid the guest of honor feeling embarrassed or at a disadvantage—as she sits in her running gear amid a crowd attired in summer dresses.

One final precaution about surprise showers. People love to give them, but not everyone loves to be surprised. In other words, it is best to keep the wishes of the person being honored in mind when planning a party. If the bride hates surprises, tell her of your wish to give her a shower. It will make your planning easier, for you can consult with her, and it will allow her to prepare herself.

When planning a shower, be sure that anyone who is invited will also be invited to the wedding, since it is inconsiderate to ask people to a preliminary party but not the main event. This is particularly easy to coordinate if the bride is consulted about the guest list. The only acceptable exception to the rule is when friends would like to honor the bride or groom but the wedding is to be very small with only family attending.

Plan the shower as you would any other party (see chapter 2), choosing a theme, guest list, menu, and then preparing for it. Showers are usually given at home. Depending on the kind of party, you may wish to use your living room, den, or yard. Similarly, the food might be simple or elaborate, the drink punch, wine, or cocktails. You may wish to set a buffet table with an arrangement of flowers, tablecloth and napkins in the bride's favorite color, and your best china and silver, or use place mats, your stoneware, and stainless.

Whatever the kind of party and the theme, showers are an opportunity for the friends of the bride and groom to get together and share in the excitement before the wedding.

The Rehearsal Dinner

The eve of a wedding is a cause for celebration—most often a dinner that follows the rehearsal for the members of the wedding party. Rehearsal dinners may also include other members of the family or guests who have come from out of town. These dinners, usually given by the family of the groom if the bride's family is giving the wedding, provide an opportunity for the families to meet and celebrate the coming event. It's a time for sentimental speeches and funny anecdotes in an atmosphere of anything from a formal dinner to a family supper.

A rehearsal dinner given at home is a perfect chance to create an atmosphere that is both warm and festive. An elegant evening can be created by setting the table with white linen and the best china, crystal, and silver. A candlelit table and rooms full of flowers help provide a blend of both the appropriate seriousness and the joy that weddings represent. The guests should be seated according to a prearranged plan in order for the disparate elements to meet and mingle. An elegant meal arrives on command, served by silent waiters and waitresses, freeing the hostess to both entertain and be entertained.

A more casual event can be created at home if it's more to your taste or budget. Flowers and soft lights once again help create a romantic aura, but this time a buffet table set with pretty dishes of food and lit with candles makes an elegant but less formal statement. The hostess makes up a seating plan if she has enough table space to seat guests (people are much more comfortable eating from a table than from their laps), but guests help themselves to food. In the wintertime, a big tureen of soup or stew can anchor a simple meal featuring only bread, salad, and dessert. In the spring or summer, a cold sliced roast or chicken dish or a main-course salad could be the meal's centerpiece. Whatever the food and atmosphere created, the party should have some special element, be it the decorations, food, or drink that stands out and gives guests the feeling that they are part of a joyous event.

A casual yet stylish rehearsal dinner can be held almost anywhere—even on the beach. For one such event the wedding was to be very small and all the guests were from out of town, including the bride and groom. Everyone was given instructions to arrive on the eve of the wedding at a precise spot on the beach just before sunset. When guests arrived, they found a big bonfire surrounded by huge logs, with a card table set up as a bar on one side and a food table on the other. As people gathered, they congregated near the fire, admiring the sunset to the accompaniment of the

A lovely Serenade fragrance bottle makes the perfect gift for the bride's attendants.

rumbling surf. Everyone had something to talk about—the wedding, the setting, the travel.

The meal, provided by a local caterer, was simple picnic food. People ate grilled fish, barbecued chicken, and hot dogs, potato salad, tossed green salad, and brownies for dessert. Then everyone stayed and talked until the wee hours, generations meeting new generations, all strangers gathered for a specific joyous event becoming friends. It was a great way to begin a full wedding weekend.

Sometimes in the course of wedding preparations people's emotions become rather frayed, particularly since everyone involved seems to have a fixed idea about the only right way to handle some aspect of the wedding. Therefore, a few guidelines about rehearsal dinners many be useful.

When planning a rehearsal dinner, plan a party that is in keeping with the wedding. A very formal dinner given before a casual outdoor wedding might unfairly focus attention away from the wedding. On the other hand, don't feel you must give a party that is completely out of character for you just to meet the style of the bride and groom and their wedding. If your style is homey and warm and the wedding cool and official, you might consider taking the party to a more neutral place, perhaps a restaurant that fits somewhere in between the two styles.

Choose a budget that is comfortable for you and tailor the party to meet it. If you can afford only twenty people, make such limitations clear to the bride and groom, who are apt to lose their heads a bit as the wedding nears and invite everyone in sight. Compromises can be easily reached as well. Perhaps the groom dreams of a raw bar of clams and oysters on the half shell at the party, but the expense of it means you can't invite some people important to your son, the bride, or you. Maybe the groom can be persuaded to save his seafood extravaganza for the honeymoon.

Rehearsal Dinner Customs

Rehearsal dinners invariably feature a wealth of toasts. Some are to the bride, others to the couple. It is a time when people are apt to make spontaneous short speeches and recite specially written poems and limericks. Reminiscences and funny stories are often told about the groom.

Remember when you find yourself toasted from the engagement party on through the big day that everyone except the person (or persons) being honored drinks after the toast is given. The bride or the couple, if the toast is to them both, smile graciously but refrain from imbibing. To drink would be to honor yourself.

Inviting the Guests

■

1. *Before you begin making your lists, set a budget for the event, which will tell you how many guests you can invite.*

2. *Start with the premise that half of the invitations are for the groom and his family and half for the bride and hers.*

3. *Who should be invited? Immediate family members of both sides and the wedding party obviously are the first considerations. Godparents, more distant relatives, and close friends of the bride and groom and their parents come next. Close business associates follow. Once you have these down you can expand to other friends and relations.*

4. *If your list becomes too long, cut it back, sending those you must leave out an announcement after the wedding, if you wish. People often send announcements to acquaintances who they would like to inform.*

5. *Expect that some people—usually about 10 percent of those you invite—will be unable to attend. If you wish, it is a nice gesture to send an invitation to people even if you know they will not be able to come.*

6. *Have your invitations printed, addressed, and ready to mail four to eight weeks before the wedding. Allow eight weeks when the wedding is during particularly busy months, such as June and December.*

7. *An invitation requires a timely response by the recipient. An invitation in itself does not require the recipient to send a gift, but it is bad manners to attend the wedding and not send or bring a gift.*

8. *An announcement does not require either a response or a gift. Recipients, however, may send a note or a gift if they wish.*

The smallest details carry the romance of a wedding, such as this balance of a perfectly decorated cake, gleaming polished silver, and crisply starched napkins.

The rehearsal dinner is also the time to give the wedding attendants gifts, unless you have a bridesmaids' luncheon and a groom's dinner. Appropriate gifts include personal objects such as jewelry for the bride's attendants and cuff links or wallets for groomsmen. Sometimes, particularly in the case of groomsmen's gifts, a thoughtful but more practical gift is welcomed. For instance, good pocket knives are often greatly appreciated. A stylish and practical gift—guaranteed to be appreciated—is crystal barware. Bridesmaids often welcome a lovely perfume bottle or piece of crystal or china giftware. The maid of honor and best man's presents are often a slightly more elaborate version of the other attendants' gifts. You need not give everyone the exact same thing, if you know each person's preferences. The trick is to give something that everyone would like that is thoughtful and of roughly equal value.

Sometimes the wedding attendants give the bride and groom special gifts at this time as well.

Since a gift from the bride or groom is meant to be a personal remembrance of the event, you don't have to follow the traditional path. One bride had only one attendant, who was immersed in the refinishing of a good amount of furniture. The bride chose an electric sanding machine. The unusual gift came off as a great joke but has served its recipient well.

Wedding Receptions

A wedding is without a doubt one of life's most important events. For lots of people it is the culmination of years of dreaming. Many women, and men too, begin in childhood to imagine their weddings.

Some of us envision ourselves in yards of silk with a ten-foot train held by tiny bearers; we walk down the aisle of a flower-laden church on our father's arm to the waiting Prince Charming. Perhaps your vision is of a wedding at home in the garden amid a bower of flowers. For some, the perfect wedding is in a meadow or on the seashore with a small band of well-wishers grouped around.

In short, a wedding and reception should be what the bride and groom want it to be. It can be a weekend event that seems to move from one party to the next, or it can be a simple civil ceremony followed by a small luncheon or cake-and-champagne reception after work. But all weddings have one thing in common: they are a time of joy and celebration, and every one has that certain something that makes it special.

The lovely reception that followed the wedding of one couple was held at the bride's parents' house. The ceremony had taken place in a nearby church, and the fifty guests were able to walk back to the bride's parents' house, a short distance away. There they found a veritable block party about to commence. The reception was set up in the two small but well-groomed backyards of the bride's parents and their next-door neighbors.

The bride, her sisters, and a few old friends had made all of the food, which started with cold finger food and later featured a full buffet. The hors d'oeuvres included delicious pastry puffs filled with cheeses, prosciutto-wrapped breadsticks, and lots of vegetables displayed on trays lined with fresh herbs. These trays were placed on tables covered with yellow cloths and decorated with simple arrangements of summer flowers. A long table, placed at the back of the larger yard, served as a bar, where a bartender held forth.

A live bluegrass band entertained during the afternoon while people mingled, some seated in groupings of folding chairs placed around the yards, others standing, some dancing. College friends became reacquainted, the families visited, and everyone gushed over the bride and groom. Various relatives and friends made toasts to the couple during the course of the afternoon—some sweet and sentimental, some silly —everyone nearby participating.

Near sunset the guests were beckoned into the neighbors' house, where a buffet was served out of the dining room. The food was simple but carefully prepared and featured smoked turkey, homemade bread, a vegetable salad of summer-ripe tomatoes, another with crisp lettuce and radicchio, and pasta with pesto. The food was displayed on beautiful china and silver, the table set with lace over a yellow cloth. The centerpiece was an extravagant collection of summer flowers from the garden. Candles lit the room.

Once served, the guests seated themselves in groups inside the house or out on the lawns, where tables and chairs awaited. After dinner everyone gathered on the porch to witness the bride and groom cutting the wedding cake, which was decorated with fresh garden flowers. More toasts were made, champagne drunk, and the cake with ice cream eaten.

A reminder of the day's events, a bride's bouquet featuring white lilies.

The guests made their way home gradually, many carrying their sleeping children, and the music finally stopped.

Since everything was done by the bride and her family, the planning was pretty detailed. They began about two months ahead, deciding on the menu, assigning people to make certain dishes, checking lists, reserving the musicians. They ordered the cake a month ahead of time and arranged to rent chairs and tables about three weeks in advance. They began the preparation of the food about three days before the wedding—setting up work teams in various kitchens. So while the party looked effortless, it was really quite efficiently ordered.

Another festive wedding was held in the meadow of the bride's grandmother's house in Massachusetts. The house, modest in size and design, sits at the top of a gently sloping hill amid fifty acres of beautiful open meadow. The wedding was planned for a sunny weekend in June so that it could take place out-of-doors. But as the day approached—and after several weekends of rain—the bride and her family became nervous and investigated renting tents. In the end they decided to place a reservation and deposit on a couple of tents and have them put up only if the forecast looked grim the day before the event.

Luckily, it was a gorgeous day as the bride emerged from her grandmother's house, wearing her mother's gown and her grandmother's veil. She glided through a formal garden and out into the meadow, where her groom and all the guests waited. After the short and simple ceremony, the family formed a receiving line in the formal garden to greet their guests. As people passed through the line, waiters bearing glasses of champagne and hors d'oeuvres circulated, serving both those assembled in the main party area and those in the receiving line. Most important, they refreshed the bridal party and families.

Once everyone had been properly greeted, the families began circulating. After a short while, everyone was seated for a luncheon served by a catering staff. The tables were covered with pink cloths that reached nearly to the ground. They were simply decorated with vases of wildflowers, picked from the meadow itself—bachelor's buttons, Queen Anne's lace, and other greenery made for a handsome display.

The meal itself was simple, too, consisting of a cold cucumber soup, seafood salad, steamed vegetables, and fruit. After the meal, the soft music changed tempo so everyone could dance. After the bride and her father started, everyone gradually joined in. As the afternoon wound down to sunset, the guests drifted away.

The Etiquette of Wedding Gifts

■

Giver

1. Gifts that seem generous but within your means are always appreciated. Don't feel the need to impress.

2. Try to make sure the gift arrives at the bride's, or her parents', house before the wedding. To have it arrive after the wedding looks as though you judged the gift by how much you enjoyed the wedding. To take it to the wedding looks as though you are bringing an entrance fee.

3. Try to find out what the couple would like as a gift. One way to be sure is to check local department store bridal registries. Sending a gift that the couple has listed ensures that your gift will be right on target.

4. Be sure to enclose a card with your gift, and make sure it is secured to the package or wrapped inside.

Bride and Groom

1. Record the receipt of each gift.

2. Do not open gifts at the wedding unless it is a small family affair.

3. Write a personal note thanking each person who gave a gift. When people take the time and trouble to choose a gift, the least you can do is thank them personally.

4. Refer to the gift specifically in the note.

5. Send thank-you notes promptly. People will be anxious to know if their gift was received.

General

You need not send a gift if you choose not to attend a wedding.

A Note about Bridal Registries

■

As the wedding approaches, people will begin asking what you would like for wedding gifts. To prepare for this, sit down and think through your needs. Choose china, crystal, and silverware patterns. Consider your needs for linens and other household goods. Be sure to choose gifts in a wide range of prices. When your list is complete, register your choices with the bridal department of at least one store.

Then when someone asks you, "What would you like?" you can gracefully answer, "Well, I'm registered at Hall's."

For the guest, working through the bridal registry is the easiest way to buy a gift for a number of reasons. First, you are assured that the gift will be exactly what the bride and groom want and need. Second, you need not worry about duplicating gifts, since the registry records all gifts ordered. Third, the store handles the wrapping, packing, and delivering of the gift. Finally, if for any reason the gift does not meet the bride and groom's needs, it can be returned easily.

There it is, the classic tiered wedding cake, elegantly decorated.

Not all small and simple weddings need to be done at your own home to be effective. At one delightful wedding, the guests gathered from up and down the Eastern seaboard at an island off the Virginia coast for what was for everybody an out-of-town wedding. The groom's family's rented vacation house served as the focus for the weekend events.

The traditional wedding took place in a tiny Victorian Carpenter Gothic-style church on the mainland at eleven in the morning. The bride wore a white cotton tea-length dress and carried white flowers. The groom wore a blue blazer and light slacks. The bride had one attendant, and the groom's tiny nieces acted as flower girls, stealing the show by happily—and quite unselfconsciously—chattering throughout the service. After the wedding, the families formed a receiving line on the church lawn so that everyone could be greeted officially. The bride and groom then formed the head of a procession in their open-topped jeep that traveled back to the island for a wedding brunch at home.

Back at the house, a local catering crew was preparing the last touches for a seafood buffet. When the wedding couple and guests arrived, they entered the house to find trays of champagne. After a toast or two, they proceeded out to the large screened porch that overlooked the water. The porch was set with a long T-shaped table. At the far end of the porch was the buffet table, where the catering staff presided. Each guest passed through the line and, upon finding his or her place card, sat down at the long table. The bride and groom, their attendants, and parents took the head table that formed the top of the T. The tables were decorated with summer flowers in shades of pink, in low arrangements so that people could see one another across the table. That wedding was at once a very traditional, formal affair, yet enhanced by the informal air of the resort town in which it was held.

The Postwedding Party at Home

Most people do not have the space to give large weddings at home. As a result, it is not unusual for the bride's family to have a party at home after the reception. For many, this is the party at which everyone relaxes and has time to visit.

Often the bride and groom, if they haven't left for a honeymoon trip, will attend these warm and intimate parties. They may be having so much fun that they don't want the party to end and welcome the relaxed postwedding party at a parents' house.

Forming a Receiving Line
■

A receiving line is an easy and efficient method for greeting wedding guests and it's very simple to do. The people who must be included are the bride's mother, the groom's mother, and the bride and groom. Fathers often join the receiving line, since they are as involved in their children's weddings as their wives, but they can mingle with the guests if they wish. Attendants may also join the line, but since it's often hard for them to make conversation with guests they haven't met before, they need not join. This is the order of the receiving line:

1. Mother and father of the bride
2. Mother and father of the groom
3. Bride and groom
4. Maid of honor
5. Bridesmaids

The Bride's Table
■

When a seated meal forms the focus of a wedding reception, the bride and groom and their attendants are seated at a rectangular table of their own. They are seated on one side only to allow the guests to see the bride and groom. The bride and groom sit in the middle of the table, the bride seated to the groom's left. The best man sits on her left and the maid of honor on the groom's right. The bridesmaids and ushers alternate to the right and left of the couple. If there is still room, close friends or family are seated at the head table as well.

A wedding dinner offers the ideal opportunity for setting an elegant table. CHINA: *Lowell* CRYSTAL: *Charleston*

These parties can range from the very simple to the very elegant, depending on your preference. They are usually cocktail parties or cocktail buffets, but can be backyard picnics or formal dances. Since such a party serves as a wind-down, a postwedding party should seem unharried, and, as usual, the best way to achieve this is through careful advance planning. The party need not be elaborate—actually, it shouldn't be, since the wedding and reception are the key events. But the house should be prepared to receive guests and arrangements should be made for food and drink.

Food is most welcome at such parties. The families of the bride and groom, busy as the social focus of the event, may have missed out on the food at the reception. Platters of sliced meat, pâtés, and salads or other simple dishes made in advance work nicely, as they can be ready to be put out when guests arrive. Sometimes extra platters of hors d'oeuvres are sent home from the reception. It's more important to provide a full range of beverages at the afterparty than at the reception, since people will be relaxing and are likely to be thirsty for everything from coffee and diet soda to champagne or cocktails.

As for decorating the house, you might elect to bring the flower arrangements from the reception. They make a nice transition and keep the theme of the wedding. These can be messengered by family members or ushers sent on ahead. Flowers for the table should be arranged specially by the florist and delivered in advance so that the table is set and ready to go when the first guest arrives.

The house should be ready to receive guests. Plan as you might, the hours right before a wedding are likely to be hectic, so consider hiring someone to be at home making the preparations for the party, such as doing a last-minute pickup, setting the table, and preparing the bar. This person is also invaluable during the party to keep platters filled and glasses cleared and to finally clean up, allowing family members to socialize and relax without having to worry about the dishes.

With these few steps taken you can come to your own party and enjoy it thoroughly as hostess or host—and thus round out a great event.

Inviting close friends and family back to the house for a simple postwedding party is a great way to wind down the festivities. The mood tends to be easy and guests have a real chance to visit. CHINA: *Monroe* CRYSTAL: *Classic Regency*

Celebrating Anniversaries and Birthdays

Whether we like it or not, birthdays and anniversaries mark the linear progression of our lives. Chances are good that the first of such celebrations precedes our births, as many of our mothers were honored with a baby shower. Next comes the first birthday party, though it's really a party for our parents, celebrating the changing of their lives as much as marking our growth.

Later on, birthday parties play an important role in our growing awareness of the world. We mark subsequent years, too, especially those associated with certain rites of passage. Sixteen is a big year, the one in which we can first drive a car. Coming of age at twenty-one is another significant one—the last one we see as dependents of our parents. After that our milestone birthdays are further apart: thirty, forty, fifty, seventy-five, eighty.

The other important yearly celebration is the wedding anniversary. Most anniversaries are celebrated rather privately by the couple, perhaps with an evening on the town or a romantic dinner for two at home. Anniversaries that mark certain years provide opportunities for more public celebrations. Tenth, twenty-fifth, fortieth, and fiftieth anniversaries are frequently celebrated with fanfare, although any anniversary warrants a party for those who wish it.

A Romantic Dinner for Two

An intimate dinner for two can be created for almost any reason, but it's a great idea for a wedding anniversary, be it the first or the fifty-first. For some people such a private celebration turns into a tradition, often repeated at Valentine's Day. Such evenings can be an opportunity to create a special event for a loved one that focuses on the interests and desires of just the two of you, apart from the general concerns of family life. If you have small children, they can be sent to a sitter. If your children are teenagers, pack them off to the movies or to their friends for an overnight stay.

Anniversaries, birthdays, and weddings are opportunities to give beautiful personal yet useful gifts. CHINA: *Charleston vase*

If you have sufficient free time and like to cook, make this an opportunity to indulge yourself in creating a special, time-consuming meal. If you don't care much for cooking or are too busy, you can always use a combination of simple easy-to-prepare dishes. It all depends on your and your spouse's tastes. In some people's eyes there is nothing more romantic than oysters on the half shell—cool, briny oysters on a bed of ice garnished with wedges of lemon. They are easy to prepare, too, since they require no cooking—just a strong hand for opening. For others romance is symbolized by a bowl of caviar surrounded with toast points and served with a glass of champagne or slices of smoked salmon on brown bread with butter. A simple broiled lamb chop or fish or perhaps a bowl of steamed mussels are other easy and delectable choices. Maybe it's the time to make a spouse's favorite dishes. Whatever you choose, make sure that the food serves to highlight the intimate atmosphere, yet is not so fussy that you find yourself preoccupied with its preparation.

The table should be laid with care. This is a great time to use your best china, silver, and crystal to lift the evening out of the ordinary. They can be placed on attractive place mats or a formal tablecloth. The napkins should be cloth and as luxurious as you have. Place the settings fairly close together—not suffocatingly so, but not miles away, either.

Whatever you choose to use, make the table and setting special. Plan the lighting so that it is soft and flattering. Remove the baby's high chair. While you're at it, remove all the other chairs, too. Bring out a special vase or decorative piece that you haven't used in years because it seemed too precious or too silly. After all, a romantic dinner doesn't have to be serious.

A romantic dinner should be relaxed and unhurried, so take things at an even pace. Set the table before the evening begins and arrange the meal so that it requires only a small amount of preparation before serving. If at all possible, try to organize it well enough that you have a little time to pamper yourself before dinner. Before dressing, take a bath or a fifteen-minute rest to relax. Then, when the evening begins, you are already in a leisurely mood, confident that everything is in hand.

———————————————

Oysters on the half shell are a perfect first course for an intimate dinner for two. CHINA: *Royal Peony* CRYSTAL: *Classic Laurel; Charleston salt and pepper set and candlesticks*

The Anniversary Party

The evening began at the apartment of the host, where a couple arrived for what they thought would be a small celebration. They were surprised as numerous friends, sleekly dressed in evening clothes (as were they), began arriving at the apartment.

Soon the place was quite crowded. Champagne flowed into crystal flutes, toasts were made, and presents, all of them tin, were opened. Then everyone spilled downstairs to waiting limousines. A true night on the town ensued, beginning with a Russian nightclub and ending in the wee hours of the morning at an after-hours jazz club. At dawn the guests were deposited on their own doorsteps. That was a tin anniversary that everyone remembers as a wonderful time. The tenth anniversary, like the first, twenty-fifth, fortieth, and fiftieth, among others, seems to carry more weight than others. The longer you've been married, the more public anniversaries become, too.

Yet some people prefer not to celebrate their anniversaries. One couple never made much of theirs. At the fortieth anniversary celebration of Ann's brother, she turned to one of her sons and said, "Did you know this is our fortieth anniversary, too?" He didn't. Moreover, for another nine years it remained Ann and Philip's private day, but for their fiftieth their children gave them an afternoon reception at which over fifty of their friends came to wish them well. They took the party in good spirit, not seeming to mind that such an uncharacteristic fuss was made—they even enjoyed themselves.

People love to give special anniversary parties—either for themselves or for their parents. They can be large parties or small, depending on your preference. When planning such a party, it is often helpful to keep a few things in mind. First, people who give parties for others seem to assume that a big anniversary party should be a surprise. Sometimes this is the perfect thing, sometimes not. If the principals really do not appreciate surprises, include them in the planning. You will not only make your own planning easier, since you can ask them what they would like and who they would like to see, but then they can share in the excitement of the planning. Another tactic to use is to slyly let them know to expect something.

Another kind of party is the one that the couple gives themselves. Some couples use such parties as an opportunity to gather the participants in their wedding and renew their vows. This can be done with a clergyman present or more informally.

Anniversary parties range from afternoon receptions at someone's home to dinner

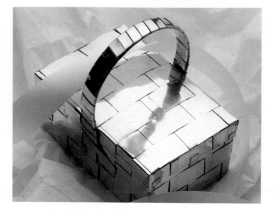

This woven basket makes an ideal party favor for a silver wedding celebration.

Mementos

■

Big anniversary parties also provide an opportunity for using personalized mementos as part of the decoration. Traditional choices include coasters, match covers, and cocktail and luncheon-sized napkins with the name of the couple and their wedding date and the years married, such as:

Harry and Louise
May 29
1940–1990

Providing favors as mementos is another nice touch. Splits of champagne, tiny nosegays of flowers, or a boxed piece of wedding cake for continued good luck make charming mementos.

A tiny nosegay of dried or fresh flowers makes a charming decoration and party favor.

and dancing at a club. When planning an anniversary party at home, you can choose between an afternoon reception—often the best when people have been married fifty years or more, since many of their friends have given up driving at night—and an evening dinner party or a cocktail reception.

Decorating for special anniversaries can provide an opportunity to use the family memory bank, since you can draw from the couple's experience. For instance, use the color scheme of the original wedding for the table linens, flowers, balloons, and other decorations. You can also use wedding or courting photos of the couple in a number of ways. You can have them blown up poster size, or put them in frames and arrange them on a table to form a narrative, or scatter them around the house. You can also make an attractive collage of photos showing the couple and their family and friends over the years.

If you prefer more traditional decorations, certain anniversaries, such as silver and gold, have automatic color schemes. A buffet table set with white or yellow flowers and silver or gold ribbons looks beautiful with pretty china and gleaming crystal and silverware.

Wedding cake is the traditional dessert at anniversary parties, but beyond that the kind of party will dictate the offerings. Ann and Phil's afternoon reception featured light hors d'oeuvres and vegetables with dips, cold cuts and rolls, and an assortment of pies (Phil's favorite kind of dessert) and wedding cake. An evening cocktail party might feature hot hors d'oeuvres or a complete dinner buffet including an entree or two, vegetables, salads, fruit, and wedding cake. Plenty of iced champagne should be on hand.

When planning an anniversary party, don't forget the music. Such a party is a terrific opportunity to bring out the oldies and play the music of the couple's youth. A live combo can take requests and play the couple's favorites, but plenty of records or a few good tapes prepared in advance make excellent second choices. If you plan to play dance music, remember to leave space for people to dance.

Anniversary Gifts

When planning an anniversary party you will inevitably face the question of gifts. Your guests will want to know the right thing to do. Are presents encouraged or not, and, if so, what should people give?

Couples who have been married only a short time often still need things, in which case it is appropriate for them to be given something useful that they will like. People

Traditional Anniversaries

■

1. *Paper*	13. *Lace*
2. *Cotton*	14. *Ivory*
3. *Leather*	15. *Crystal*
4. *Silk*	20. *China*
5. *Wood*	25. *Silver*
6. *Iron*	30. *Pearl*
7. *Copper or wool*	35. *Coral or jade*
8. *Bronze or pottery*	40. *Ruby*
9. *Willow or pottery*	45. *Sapphire*
10. *Tin or aluminum*	50. *Gold*
11. *Steel*	55. *Emerald*
12. *Linen or silk*	60. *Diamond*

Sometimes a small personal gift is just the ticket to show someone you care. You might want to say thank you for a lovely weekend or offer a token of your affection for Valentine's Day, a birthday, anniversary, or other special day. SHOWN: *Rose Manor fragrance bottle,* right

Everybody knows about celebrating fiftieth anniversaries with gold and twenty-fifths with silver, but others have symbols, too. For instance, people might give this little Mexican tin mirror, center, *as a favor at a tenth anniversary party.*

A tin toy is a fun and thoughtful token present, far right, *for a couple's tenth anniversary.*

who have been married a long while usually have everything they need, and so it becomes more difficult.

The traditional gifts for people married twenty-five years involve something silver, and for fifty years, something gold. This does not obligate anyone to give precious metals. In fact, one is not required to give any gift at all. Many longtime married couples prefer no presents and if given the opportunity would tell you they prefer your company to any gift, or they may even request that no presents be given. Formally asking that gifts not be brought presents a problem because it looks as though someone is expecting a guest to give a present when such occasions do not require them. Some people will be grateful for the request, others will feel awkward. If you feel such a request is necessary, word it gracefully with a phrase like "The pleasure of your company would be the greatest gift."

If gifts are appropriate, they don't have to be silver or gold, rubies or pearls. How about a flower arrangement or an unusual plant for the garden, a bottle of good wine, theater tickets, or a photo album to be filled with pictures of the party? For those closely related, a homemade videotape chronicling the couple's years together —beginning with their wedding photos and including shots of places they've lived

and interviews with children and friends—can provide a tangible memento of the love and devotion lavished on them. One delightful gift is a signature quilt, made by someone special to the guests of honor and autographed by everyone who attends the party.

A Baby Shower

The arrival of a baby is a source of great joy, often celebrated with a shower either before the baby is born or after. The principal purpose of a baby shower is to provide the new parents with the necessities of family life. Baby showers are more often than not still ladies-only occasions, the theory being that men feel uncomfortable around discussions of clothing, feeding, and diapers. This, of course, is gradually changing as men become more involved in child care.

The party opportunities for a baby shower have been evolving too, as women's careers have become more varied. It used to be that baby showers were given in the afternoon or early evening and featured dessert and coffee. While they are still simple parties, these days more showers are given after work or on weekends and serve a simple meal or feature wine and cheese or champagne (or sparkling nonalcoholic cider) and dessert.

One agreeable format for a baby shower is a weekend brunch given by a close friend, which gathers people for a simple party that provides sustenance. Spouses can be invited or not, as the hostess wishes. Such a party can be a large buffet or a small seated meal, depending on the number of people attending. At a brunch you can serve a hot egg dish or sandwiches and salads along with coffee cake or bagels and cream cheese.

The table, either for a seated meal or buffet, can be set with pastel-colored linens, streamers, and flowers with china that coordinate. People often decorate using pastel pink, blue, and yellow for a baby theme.

An informal buffet is a particularly good method for serving food. Since guests sit at random, the attention is focused on the main business at hand: the opening of the gifts. Also, as the presents are being opened, guests can refill a cup of coffee or pick up a handful of grapes during the lulls in the action when everyone admires each present.

Scheduling a baby shower can be tricky. If you plan a shower in advance of the

Celebrating the imminent arrival of a baby with a simple brunch provides an opportunity to congregate and share a light meal. CHINA: *Chinastone Glories on Gray* CRYSTAL: *Atrium, Optika bowl*

baby's birth, it's usually safe to schedule it in the seventh or eighth month. The expectant mother should feel well enough to come and should be far enough in advance of the due date that if the baby elects to arrive a little early you won't have to reschedule the shower until after the birth. Also, try to find out what time of day the expectant mother feels best and try to schedule the party for then, if convenient.

Gifts

Baby presents tend to be practical, since babies require so many clothes and special articles. This doesn't mean that adorable baby china or a silver mug will not be appreciated. They can even be considered practical, since silver mugs are unbreakable and china ones can either be used with care or passed along when the child is older and understands the appeal of the gift. Such gifts are also the sorts of things that can be passsed from generation to generation. A savings bond falls into this general category, too. It may not keep the child in diapers, but it will be appreciated in the years to come.

As far as other baby presents go, the field is fairly broad. Clothing is always appropriate, since babies need quantities of it. Choose large sizes, since even a small baby will grow into them. All-purpose receiving blankets and crib blankets and quilts are useful. Mobiles, infant activity boxes, and stuffed animals are popular. Books on babies, both useful and humorous, make good presents as well. Cooperating on a large present of the parents' preference, such as a stroller, carrying pack, or other expensive piece of equipment is a good way for people to provide something that might be a financial strain on the new parents. Unless the sex of the baby is known and has been announced in advance, try to choose gifts that are neutral.

Children's Birthday Parties

Everyone remembers their favorite childhood birthday party, the one to which the whole school class was invited so no one would feel left out. It was a glorious party, with cake and punch and favors for everyone.

The event of the afternoon may have been the entertainment, perhaps hitting a beautiful piñata made in the shape of a star or circus animal. Everyone had a turn

If the table is messy, the children had a good time. CHINA: *Teacher's Pets*

trying to break open the colorful papier-mâché treasure trove as it moved up and down on a rope maneuvered by a brother. Finally, on the second or third round, it burst, throwing toys and little wrapped candies all over the room while every child scrambled for a share. It was a great party, not only because you were the lucky birthday kid, but because everyone had a role in the main event. Sure, opening the presents was fun, but the piñata was exotic and colorful.

Children's birthday parties generally work best when they are fairly simple. The food can be just ice cream and cake with milk or punch or, depending on the time of day, a little more elaborate, featuring, for example, a sandwich or hot dog at lunchtime. Parties for children under the age of six should be fairly short. One to two hours is plenty. Parties for older children can stretch up to about three hours before everyone—adults as well as children—becomes tired.

Popular entertainments at children's parties include traditional children's games, hired performers such as magicians and clowns, and creative activities such as baking birthday cookies, making ice cream, and folding and decorating party hats and toys. When the kids begin to tire, videotapes of children's movies or cartoons are a great way to calm down.

Theme parties can be great fun. Traditional subjects include clowns and circus animals, cowboys and Indians, ballerinas, and princesses. Current ones include sports figures and cartoon and fantasy characters. Children are often encouraged to bring their favorite toys to share and come as their favorite character, which can be amusing when five boys sporting Superman capes swoop around. Children aren't the only ones who can dress up, as parents often enjoy getting suited up too and acting in theme.

The table at a birthday party usually is a focus of attention, since it is the home of the all-important cake. It is thus the place where most of the party decorations are found. Everyone responds with delight to seeing bright balloons (indeed, for many of all ages they are essential birthday decorations). Blowers and inflated balloons set at each place are great fun, as are party hats and even noisemakers (depending on your sensitivity). Party favors placed at each spot are always a good idea. Party favors in some form, perhaps a small game, toy, piece of jewelry, or other treat, are essential so that all the children—not only the birthday boy or girl—will have something to take home.

As for the children, the junior host or hostess should begin training in the art of party-giving early. The birthday child is the host or hostess of the party and as such has certain simple responsibilities.

A colorful piñata makes a great game at a birthday party. Everyone joins in trying to split it open, then dashes for the prizes held within.

A child's birthday cake, top, *can be an opportunity for a little freewheeling fun, like these foil-covered chocolate cars racing on a track of red licorice shoelaces.*

Confetti and streamers, above, *are a sure sign of a high-spirited party.*

At children's birthday parties, right, *hot dogs and milk shakes are as popular as ice cream and cake.* CHINA: *Teacher's Pets* CRYSTAL: *Antique iced beverage*

The birthday child should greet each and every guest, thank each one for the present given, and also say good-bye. The guests in turn have the responsibility of greeting the host or hostess and the mother or father and thanking the same people for having invited them when they leave. Aside from these specific duties, all you can do is hope that the manners you have painstakingly taught are remembered.

Coming-of-Age Dinners

There are at least two times of coming of age—one when you turn sixteen and feel that you've done all the growing up that needs to be done, the other when you turn twenty-one and actually reach the age of majority. Both are important stages of life and often are celebrated with dinners.

At sixteen the party can be an approximation of an adult dinner. One convinces one's mother to bring out the good china and a nice tablecloth and to fix the favorite meal or even to prepare something exotic and particularly "adult," such as lobster bisque.

Perhaps the sixteen-year-old invites four or five best friends over and presumes that candlelit dinners with nice china and flowers are his or her due. The conversation, of course, centers on who already has their drivers' license, who is getting it tomorrow, and who is dating whom. Other topics naturally include school—how it's going now and who will be going where in two years. If it is a birthday party, presents are given, just as at a normal family party, with the vain hope that Dad will surprise you with a set of car keys.

If the sixteenth birthday party was the dry run for an adult party, the twenty-first is the real thing. When you turn twenty-one you are acknowledged to have officially entered adulthood. Coming-of-age dinners are often family parties with a few outsiders, such as particularly close friends and, of course, current amours.

Here again, the party provides an opportunity for creating a grown-up setting, using fine linen, the best china, crystal, and silver amid the soft light of candles and the beauty of fresh flowers. Dinner may be the center of attention's favorite meal (probably more sophisticated than the sixteen-year-old's menu), and now that he or she is an adult, probably at least partially prepared by the honored guest. Sentimental and inspiring speeches have been known to be given as well as gifts (although this time the fantasy may involve the parents handing over the keys to an apartment rather than just the car). Toasts are made, often with the first official champagne or wine of adulthood.

The favorite food for a sixteenth birthday might be the classic burger and fries. For a twenty-first? It might be lobster thermidor. CHINA: Jefferson CRYSTAL: Allure

Holiday Parties

There is no law, written or otherwise, that says you have to have an excuse to entertain. On the other hand, there is no better reason to have a party than a fully sanctioned old-fashioned holiday.

Holidays are times when sharing with friends and relatives seems to come naturally. Tradition has it that the holiday season runs from Thanksgiving to New Year's, yet we also celebrate Valentine's Day, Easter or Passover, July Fourth, and Labor Day, with other holidays sandwiched in between. Then our extended holiday season takes a short rest until Thanksgiving—which is where we begin our year's worth of holiday parties.

Thanksgiving Dinner

Thanksgiving is all about family and friends in a mutual celebration of that Puritan harvest back in the seventeenth century, and all of those before and since for which we give thanks. And, like any holiday, it demands tradi-

tions, usually ones that each family develops over the years.

We begin with the certain cultural given, turkey. Turkey is the national symbol of Thanksgiving, and those who don't serve it are renegades forging their own traditions. So they should, if they wish, but for most red-blooded Americans roast turkey is the dish of the day. Cranberries in some form and pumpkin pie are other usual accompaniments, but after these foods the menus vary.

Some households wouldn't consider it Thanksgiving without oyster dressing. Others serve stuffing flavored with sage or made with cornbread or sausage or apple and onion —the list is endless. People often serve sweet potatoes, but even there the variety is vast, for they can be baked, candied, souffléed, or mashed. Some like mashed Irish potatoes, others require boiled onions, some green beans or squash. Many households appease everyone's tastes by having everyone's favorite dish.

For millions of people, Thanksgiving also means foot-

Sparklers on a patriotic Independence Day cake make a brilliant statement. Just be careful of the sparkler fallout. CHINA: *Chinastone Poppies on Blue*

ball, beginning in the morning at the local high school Turkey Day Spectacular and followed by the college and professional games on television. Therein lies one of the tricky aspects of Thanksgiving—timing the dinner. Do you serve it before, after, or during halftime? How do you balance the needs of those who must watch with those who couldn't care less? How do you create good fellowship, not to mention good conversation, when there are two minutes left, the favorite team is down by three, and the turkey's on the table? With patience and fortitude, as Miss Manners says.

Since Thanksgiving is a celebration of the gifts of family and friendship, one of the most tangible ways of showing it is to invite friends who are separated from family. The tradition is so ingrained that many people whose families live far away find themselves gathering friends in similar circumstances. One couple have the most popular gala celebration around and have a quite genuine "family" of nearly twenty who come every year. They have been doing it with such success that their friends are very proprietary about their Thanksgiving dinner. They call up weeks ahead to make sure the planning is under way.

There are lessons in the party-givers' methodology that can be applied to almost any large family celebration. One of the reasons their party works so well is that everyone contributes to the dinner by bringing something. About a week before the event, the hostess calls up the guests and discusses the dinner, handing out assignments. She and her husband cook the turkey, make the gravy, and bake the desserts, all of which they are justly famous for. The rest of the meal is divvied up. One friend is assigned to bring the cranberry sauce, another a salad of his choice, another the stuffing, yet another the sweet potatoes, others the vegetables. Each person is free to make whatever dish he or she likes within the scope of the assigned food. The ones who don't cook bring wine, port, cider, nuts, or whatever they feel comfortable providing. Each year the hosts ask a few new people, too, and they're given free rein to bring what they choose. If they profess no preference for special dishes or refreshments, they are given easy assignments so they need not be embarrassed amid a group of close friends.

Thanksgiving dinner is without doubt the meal with the most traditional foods. Everyone seems to agree on the necessity of a roast turkey with stuffing, cranberries, and pumpkin in one form or another. After that the options vary: squash and sweet potatoes, creamed onions, chestnuts, and various cheeses are just a few of the popular foods. CHINA: *Autumn; Symphony bowl and salt and pepper set* CRYSTAL: *Autumn*

For the regulars it is an opportunity to display their talent with a particular dish or improve on last year's offering. One fellow tries to improve his cranberry sauce each year. No ordinary cranberry-orange for him, as he comes up with ever more imaginative additions. One year it was cranberry-blueberry-banana sauce, which the assembled company deemed a dismal but entertaining failure.

Although Thanksgiving foods tend to be traditional, there is no reason not to add something new to the lineup of standard dishes. This is what Peter of the imaginative cranberry sauce tries to do. A little excitement is welcome in almost any meal, including Thanksgiving dinner, provided it doesn't threaten to change the character of the meal for tradition-minded guests. You might try a special bread, such as a corn-cheese muffin, or a specially prepared vegetable, such as winter squash with sour cream and poppy seeds, or a variation on a favorite dessert, such as a caramelized pumpkin custard.

An issue that the thoughtful party-giver will face at one time or another, particularly at holidays, is that of how to deal with everyone's favorite dishes. One family in which each of the twenty-two members has a favorite dish that seems to them the essence of Thanksgiving relies on an indulgent Granny, who accommodates everyone, with the result that the table groans with dozens of dishes that have taken her the better part of a week to prepare. While there is nothing more luxurious than a full table, three different potato dishes and nine desserts can be a bit excessive, particularly for the person burdened with their preparation.

Another problem that often arises is that of special needs. Say your family always has a dressing made with eggs and a new family member has let it be known that not only is it the weirdest kind of stuffing he's ever heard of, but it's impossible for him to eat since he is allergic to eggs. You have to make a decision to either change your recipe or let him eat something else. In this case, another alternative is possible, and that is to make the stuffing as usual but to set aside a small amount without eggs.

For people who don't have the time or inclination to cater to every possible whim, there are better methods for dealing with favorites and special requests than preparing every dish. One method is to rotate the favorite dishes each year so that, for example, one time you serve candied sweet potatoes, another baked ones. That way everyone knows that their turn will eventually come up. Another method is to take contributions of certain dishes by asking willing cooks to make them.

Since the focus of Thanksgiving is the meal, the dinner table reflects the

Tending to the Turkey

■

If you're running your own Thanksgiving celebration for the first time, perhaps the most important thing to remember is that turkeys take a very long time to cook.

Scheduling

All of the necessary steps to preparing the meal must be scheduled early to allow time to do them easily. A carefully planned schedule should be done for all the dishes to be prepared—the bounty that serves to signify Thanksgiving usually translates to many more dishes than at a normal meal.

Preparation

A frozen turkey takes about two hours per pound to thaw in the refrigerator. Preparing it for cooking takes at least twenty minutes more. Stuffing the bird can take anywhere from twenty minutes to an hour and a half, depending on the kind of dressing you make.

Cooking

Once you reach the cooking stage, the bird requires about twenty-five minutes per pound to cook. Thus, a fresh fifteen-pound bird takes six hours to cook—a good chunk of the day. A frozen bird requires an extra day and a half of thawing.

traditions of a family almost as much as the food. Out come the big turkey platter, the heirloom silver ladle, and Great-Aunt Sarah's Army–Navy tablecloth. You can decorate the table with a cornucopia of fruit, a big bowl of fall chrysanthemums, or the little pilgrim candles the children have always loved.

Indeed, Thanksgiving centerpieces are among the most imaginative. Bouquets of autumn flowers and bunches of Indian corn, gourds, apples, and other fruits spilling from attractive containers always look appropriately colorful and seasonal. An arrangement of miniature pumpkins aligned down the center of the table or a pyramid of apples looks dramatic. A frilly purple or green-and-white flowering kale or cabbage makes a Victorian statement and looks lovely alongside heavy embroidered linen and antique lace and silver or a homespun cloth and wooden bowls.

The seating arrangement should be considered in advance. Set up conversation areas for those who like to visit, a TV area for those who want to watch the game and don't want to be disturbed. If you have two or more separate tables, avoid creating one that is the obvious winner, leaving all other guests oddly matched. The point is for everyone to have a good time, and this is usually best accomplished by spreading the guests around with an eye toward compatibility.

If your table is not large enough to seat everyone, consider seating groups of people who you know enjoy one another. If you have a large number of children, they will probably find the party more fun if they sit with one another at their own table within the view of a watchful adult or the charge of a responsible older child.

The Christmastime Cocktail Party

In many of us it's ingrained from childhood: Christmas is simply the happiest and jolliest time of the year. Even most Scrooges acknowledge that Christmas is a time of good cheer and merrymaking, a time to invite people over to share in the spirit of the season.

Cocktail parties are popular at Christmas, not least because they provide an opportunity to see a large number of friends at once, without being burdened with the elaborate preparations for a gala meal. They also provide a way to squeeze more parties into tight schedules, since people can attend more than one per evening.

A Christmas cocktail party can be given in a number of different ways. It can begin as a late weekend tea that turns into an eggnog or sherry party or it can be scheduled during the week after work. It can be formal or casual, elaborate or simple; offer a light buffet or a glass of mulled wine and a slice of fruitcake. You can serve a full bar or a specially concocted drink.

Creating a warm and welcoming atmosphere is one of the requirements of a Christmas party. One way to do this is to drape boughs of evergreens with red bows over mirrors or paintings and on mantelpieces. Another is to soften the lights and add candlelight in the evening. One gracious hostess who is famous for her Christmas parties decorates her house every year with a mass of white poinsettias lined up on a ten-foot-long bench in her living room. On her mantel she drapes evergreen swags tied with gold-lamé bows. The top of the mantel is lit with dozens of votive candles. It's a simple scheme, but one that works, since people gasp with delight as they enter the room.

Often the Christmas tree is the focus of the decorations. Whether it's a tiny-needled balsam, a feathery white pine, or a sturdy Scotch pine, every Christmas tree has its own character. And, of course, every household has its own decorating traditions. Some people like to decorate trees with themes, such as all red bows, or all white ornaments, or only edible decorations. Others collect ornaments over the years that gain sentimental connotations. The only important thing to remember about the look of the Christmas tree is that it must please you and your family.

As far as the practicality of the Christmas tree for your party, there are a few precautions to take. Make sure that the tree is firmly anchored and thus not likely to fall on someone who brushes past. Also, make sure that the ornaments likely to come in contact with milling guests are firmly secured to the tree, and, if possible, unbreakable. Guests feel terrible when an ornament falls off the tree and smashes to the floor, and so will you if the broken angel was a family heirloom. Remember, too, that all natural Christmas trees must sit in containers of water, refreshed regularly, to reduce the risk of fire hazard and to keep their lovely needles.

The practical concerns of a cocktail party can usually be anticipated in advance. One of the first elements is to determine what to serve. Will you offer a full range

---

A Christmastime party can be as simple or elaborate as you wish, from an afternoon gathering featuring food such as snacks to a dinner party offering more substantial food. CHINA: *Holiday* CRYSTAL: *Classic Laurel*

or a limited variety of drinks? If the range is wide, you will need at least one bar for a party of up to forty, and two if you have more people. If you serve a limited variety of drinks, what will you choose? Eggnog is traditional, as is glogg, mulled cider, and mulled wine. Champagne is always a festive choice.

When deciding upon the food to serve, there are a number of things to consider. One is the time of the party. If it will take place on Sunday afternoon at three, you may want to serve dessert. On Thursday at six, more substantial fare may be in order. Another element to consider is what you can manage. If you find yourself with limited time, avoid canapés that require a great deal of assembling. Instead, you might want to serve pissaladière (luscious morsels of tomatoes, spices, and cheese on crust), small pieces of quiche, and wheels of cheese with bread.

Plan the menu to include finger foods that are easy to manage without utensils and require only a cocktail napkin or perhaps a bread-and-butter plate. Good choices often include country ham, smoked turkey, or roast beef with fresh rolls or biscuits, cheese puffs, phyllo-wrapped spinach kisses, or crudités with dips. Still simpler choices might include platters of cheese and delicatessen meats with crackers and bread and simple dips with vegetables. Don't worry about your friends who are dieting. Chances are good that they are less controlled at holiday time or are able to pick and choose from among the selections offered.

The logistics of a cocktail party are also crucial. People must be able to move easily to and from the bar. The same holds true for the table holding the food. People naturally congregate around these two areas, and it will cut down congestion considerably if there are easy access routes, preferably at least two. Putting the bar in a cul-de-sac hallway is usually a mistake, as is putting it in the center of the main thoroughfare.

One method that works well to keep the party flowing is to have drinks and food passed in addition to offering them at the bar and food table. If the party is big, consider hiring people to serve so that people have food and drink available without crowding around one or two areas. Another method is to have more than one bar or food table set up.

Another concern is what crystal and china to use. If your party is large, you may not have enough glasses or small plates. Instead of resorting to plastic cups and paper plates, consider renting. It can be expensive, but having the right crystal and china will add enormously to the gracious style of the setting.

Beautiful crystal barware makes as elegant a statement as the finest stemware. CRYSTAL: *Tartan*

New Year's Day Open House

Although January sixth, known as Epiphany or Twelfth Night, officially closes the Christmas season, for most people New Year's Day marks the end of the celebration. To many people, the nicest kind of New Year's party is not a big bash to bring in the year, but a more leisurely get-together the next day.

A New Year's Day open house is a good opportunity for the hostess to show her talents. And since people may be feeling the start of postholiday letdown, it's a good time to lift spirits with an open house that is both relaxed and festive—and easy on the nerves of party-tired guests.

The menu can be simple and easy to prepare. Bloody Marys, Mimosas (champagne and orange juice), Bellinis (champagne and peach schnapps or liqueur), or plain champagne often appeal in addition to coffee, cocoa, and hot cider. Omelets made to order, flans, sliced ham, or a big pot of soup with bread, biscuits, or cornbread will provide warmth and nourishment without being too heavy. Sweet breads such as coffee cake, Danish, muffins, and panettone are welcome, as are the last Christmas desserts and a light citrus fruit salad served in crystal bowls. No matter what else you serve, a New Year's party is incomplete without black-eyed peas, the traditional southern dish meant to bring good luck in the coming year.

Casualness and effortlessness are the order of the day, although, as always, the way to make it seem easy is to plan and prepare. Make sure you have everything a day ahead, since most stores are closed on New Year's Day. Foods that can be prepared in advance help, too, so if you are serving a ham, cook it the day before and serve it cold. If making omelets, have all the ingredients out and ready to be assembled, so that you can add the personal touch to each one without having to scramble about chopping and cooking and serving—and possibly losing track and creating at least one burned omelet.

Providing entertainment is often a good idea on New Year's Day. One host has a New Year's brunch each year at which he makes waffles and sausage and lovely

---

A New Year's Day open house is an opportunity to welcome in the year with a relaxed party. No matter what you serve, be it omelets or a roast, such a gathering is incomplete without a bowl of black-eyed peas to bring luck for the year ahead. CHINA: Georgian Shell CRYSTAL: Classic Shell, Charleston candlestick, Optika candlestick

sticky sweet breads and serves orange juice and mimosas. The waffles come out of the kitchen gradually and people serve themselves from an informal buffet. After the meal everyone settles down with a cup of coffee to watch a movie on his VCR. It's always something a little sentimental. Soon everyone is misty-eyed with the movie and pleasantly lazy from the meal and the exertions of the holidays. The event has become so popular among his friends that his small living room threatens to burst into the street each year.

Valentine's Day Dinner

The most romantic of all the year's events arrives in the middle of the winter doldrums. Christmas is over and spring seems eons away, when, lo and behold, Valentine's Day slips in, bringing with it the opportunity for a fun and romantic party.

Everyone thinks of Valentine's Day as a day for lovers, but it is also a wonderful chance to entertain close friends with an unexpected bijou of an evening. Some of us have fantasies of heart-shaped cakes and a table decorated with glowing candles, red roses, and a lacy tablecloth. For those of us whose true loves think a celebration of the day consists of saying, "Oh, is it Valentine's Day?" when reminded of it, throwing a party may be the only way to realize our fantasies. It's far better to make a fun occasion by bringing in a few friends with similarly unromantic mates than to feel slighted year after year.

Bring on the elegant food, soft lights, your most beautiful china and crystal, and make a gushy evening of it. Serve things that say romance to you, such as asparagus, broiled lobster, and caviar—whatever seems indulgent and luxurious to you.

Decorate a box and ask everyone to contribute valentines to it. Make up party favors such as little baskets of Jordan almonds or tiny nosegays of flowers. Place an embroidered Valentine handkerchief or sachet at each woman's plate and a small bunch of chocolates at each man's.

Dim the lights, light scads of candles, exchange valentines, and generally indulge. It's guaranteed to lift your spirits.

What could be more romantic to close a Valentine's dinner than chocolate-dipped strawberries? CHINA: *Rose Manor heart dish*

A romantic Valentine's dinner can be a party with friends or an intimate affair just for two. Now is the time to set the table with hearts and flowers to suit the romantic theme.
CHINA: *Rose Manor* CRYSTAL: *McKinley, Charleston candlesticks, Optika oriental vase*

Easter Dinner

Spring comes at last, heralded by the celebration of Easter. Although a somber holiday at first, Easter soon becomes a celebration of life and family. For many it is often the first full gathering since Christmas. As such, like Thanksgiving and Christmas, it is bound by tradition, often including Easter baskets and dyed eggs.

The egg is the symbol of rebirth. First used in pagan spring rituals to symbolize the rebirth of the seasons, eggs have become a part of our Easter celebration. We boil them and dye them. We hide them, make nests and baskets for them, and decorate trees with them. Sometimes we dye them bright red and bake them in a braided Greek bread ring. People make cakes and cookies in the form of eggs, as well as in the shapes of other symbols of spring, such as rabbits and lambs.

Small children look forward with glee to the visit of the Easter bunny, bringing baskets of treats—usually a few dyed Easter eggs and confections such as chocolate eggs (in several forms), marshmallow bunnies and chicks, and jelly beans. It's a child's notion of nirvana.

Easter dinner is often the focus of the family celebration. Like Christmas, it has its traditional offerings. Baked ham is probably the most common entree. Next most popular in some parts of the country is roast spring lamb. After the main offering, the side dishes vary widely. Scalloped or roast potatoes set off a ham or lamb, as do new fresh peas and a green salad. A Polish Easter dinner always features ham, cabbage, in one form or another, and often babka, the tall raisin yeast cake.

The Easter table is an opportunity to show off the bounties of spring. One good way to do this is to create a light and joyous-looking table. Daffodils, tulips, and grape hyacinths make beautiful centerpiece bouquets, particularly against a white or pastel tablecloth. Arrangements of colorful eggs—hard cooked and dyed or hollow and decorated—in a frilly bowl or pastel basket always looks dramatic. You can even use inscribed dyed eggs instead of place cards. Tiny Easter baskets filled with jelly beans, chocolate eggs, and a little flower can decorate each setting.

Coloring Easter Eggs

■

Children (and adults, too) find dying Easter eggs one of the most creative and satisfying of traditions. Everyone develops his own methods, but the following are a few guidelines:

1. *Be generous with eggs. Since it can be a production getting under way, it seems more worthwhile with a gracious abundance.*

2. *Place room temperature eggs in an enamel or stainless-steel pan, cover with cool water, heat to a simmer, and cook gently for about 10 minutes. Do not boil rapidly or the shells may crack.*

3. *Cool the cooked eggs in cold water.*

4. *When ready to color the eggs, cover the table area with plenty of newspapers. Use the empty egg cartons to hold the newly colored eggs.*

5. *Use colorful crayons to decorate some of the eggs with names, bunnies, flowers, and free-form designs before dying.*

6. *For soft colors use the dyes as directed and leave the eggs in for a short time. For vivid colors, double the amount of dye and leave the eggs in for longer periods.*

7. *For an unusual look, try painting some of the eggs with dyes or watercolor paints. You can paint scenes, portraits, or even geometric or marbleized designs.*

Festive pysanki, *the intricately decorated Ukrainian Easter eggs, and parrot tulips add decorative touches to an Easter dinner.* CHINA: *Rutledge, Masterpiece vase, Symphony salt and pepper* CRYSTAL: *Classic Regency*

The Passover Seder

The other major spring holiday is Passover. Celebrated at roughly the same time as Easter, Passover is a serious but joyous eight-day festival celebrating the deliverance from Egypt of the Jewish people.

Over the centuries Passover has become a celebration of thanksgiving, spring renewal, family, and community solidarity. It is thus imbued with very strong traditions, particularly those related to the Passover seder, a special meal celebrated the first two nights of the festival at which the story of the Exodus is retold.

Certain foods play a part in the retelling of the experience of the Israelites in Egypt and are thus essential to the table. Unleavened bread, known as matzoh, symbolizes the haste in which the ancient people had to prepare their meal. Bitter herbs, usually in the form of horseradish, commemorate the bitterness of slavery. Haroset, made of a mixture of apples, raisins, nuts, and cinnamon, symbolizes the mortar the Israelites used to make bricks. Parsley and a roasted egg represent the greenery and rebirth of the seasons and are dipped in salt water to represent the tears shed by the slaves. Often a ceremonial roasted lamb shank is presented to symbolize a sacrificial lamb.

A seder table is set in a traditional manner as well, for in addition to the foods to be found, some of which are alluded to in the ceremonies, four glasses of wine are drunk, and an extra one is poured for Elijah, the prophet who is either assumed to be a guest at the party in spirit or invited but not present. The table is also often set with an extra place for Elijah and special dishes are used for the occasion.

The seder is a meal during which members of the assembled company participate in the rituals. The Passover Haggadah, a book that tells the story of the Exodus, and contains psalms, blessings, songs, and most important, the four questions, is read at various points in the meal. The four questions refer to the unique customs of Passover and are asked by the youngest member of those present.

The main course of the meal varies from house to house, but often includes

---

This Passover seder features traditional ceremonial foods: horseradish, roasted lamb shank, roasted egg, parsley, and haroset, a sweet mixture of fruits and nuts. CHINA: *Eternal; Elijah's cup, seder plate, and Sabbath candlesticks from Judaic collection; Symphony centerpiece and salt and pepper, Shelburne vase* CRYSTAL: *Classic Shell*

foods traditional to people's various backgrounds. Often chicken soup with matzoh balls, gefilte fish, boiled or baked chicken, or lamb are served. Whatever is served, however, it is the rituals of the meal that are most important—the remembrance of the past and the hope for the future.

Derby Day Celebration

Spring is really under way when the three-year-old thoroughbreds burst from the gates at Churchill Downs in Louisville, Kentucky, to compete for the coveted blanket of roses of the Kentucky Derby, the most famous race in the world. Race day is always the first Saturday in May, and in Kentucky that day is set aside as the biggest party day of the season.

If you are lucky enough to attend the Derby, you will find the women dressed in their best, complete with flowery spring hats, and men in their nattiest finery, binoculars in hand. And just about everyone will be sipping mint juleps. While most of us have to rely on television for the race itself, there is every reason to create our own mint julep party at home.

Such a party, which can be formal or informal, can be both creative and simple. You can make it as casual as asking friends to drop in for a julep around four thirty (the race coverage usually begins around five Eastern time), or you can ask everyone to dress for the occasion, the women in afternoon party dresses and hats—the bigger the better—the men in light-colored springtime suits.

A Derby Day celebration given annually by one couple varies from year to year. Sometimes friends drop in and out all afternoon, at other times the hosts make it a little more formal and set a theme. Last year everyone was asked to arrive as though they were the thoroughbred owners. The host changed from his garden clothes for the occasion and the hostess brought out a beautiful hat she had been hoping to find an occasion to wear. The guests arrived about an hour before post time to give everyone a chance to visit and to pick a horse.

One guest wrote the name of each horse on a slip of paper and put them in a

---

The Kentucky Derby is one of the surest signs of spring and a great excuse for a party. Invite some friends over, mix up mint juleps, stuff slivers of country ham into fresh biscuits, and let the festivities begin. CHINA: *Provence Green* CRYSTAL: *Charleston bowl*

hat. Everyone then anted up a dollar and pulled a slip from the hat. Serious interest in the horses developed from that point on, so that when the horses broke from the gate everyone was tense with excitement. A great hurrah rose from the holder of the winning slip. The pot was split half to the winner, with the place and show horses apportioned the remainder. Then it was back to sipping juleps and nibbling on country ham and biscuits served on small pretty plates.

The mint julep, mainstay beverage of any Derby party, requires a certain technique. First, there is the cup. Silver is the preferred material since it produces a frosty chill, but any glass or goblet works well. The cup should be chilled. Then a few tender fresh mint leaves are placed in the bottom of the cup. Next, sugar syrup is poured to taste over the leaves, then muddled with the mint with a spoon or muddler. The cup is then filled with crushed or shaved ice and a jigger of good bourbon is added. Next the mixture is stirred, a little extra bourbon is added on top, and the cup is garnished with a sprig of mint.

Sipping with a silver straw is recommended, too, although any straw will work. And keep in mind that mint juleps are pretty strong, so you probably won't have to plan on serving many refills.

Fourth of July Barbecue

The relaxed days of summer are epitomized by the celebration of Independence Day, and what better way to celebrate than with a barbecue with friends.

Picnics are, of course, portable. Even when they take place in your backyard, they should be planned for a minimum of fuss and maximum ease of serving. The ever-popular hot dogs and hamburgers are hard to beat, most especially with the younger crowd. Barbecued chicken or fish grilled over a fire appeal to almost everyone, too.

Traditional accompaniments vary widely, but often include potato salad and coleslaw. Sweet, fresh corn on the cob, perhaps the first of the season, almost guarantees a show-stopping side dish. Brownies or cookies, maybe a cake patriotically decorated with white icing and topped with strawberries or raspberries and blueberries complete the picture. A fruit salad composed of many different fruits can also be cooling and patriotically colorful. Of course, nothing beats a slice of watermelon to end the meal, complete with seed-shooting competitions for the children.

Keeping the Barbecue Safe

■

1. *Make sure that the grill is securely located on even ground.*
2. *Make sure that children are aware that a grill can be hot on the outside as well as the inside.*
3. *Set up games and play areas away from the grill.*
4. *If using an open grill, douse the fire before leaving the area. If using a covered grill, make sure the vents are closed and the top on. If your grill uses gas, make sure the gas is turned off.*
5. *Adults should serve very hot dishes to children.*

Whatever your menu, make sure that most of it is prepared ahead of time so you can relax and enjoy the festivities, whether they be volleyball, touch football, softball, swimming, or, perhaps the most satisfying of all, good conversation. You can even make a party of the preparations. Bring out the corn for shucking and in two minutes you'll have at least five people offering to strip ears. In a minute they'll be chatting and laughing and in another minute the job will be done.

The nature of the party also suggests the kind of table to set: informal. Whether you serve buffet or family style, catch the mood of the event with summer flowers, colorful place mats or tablecloth, an arrangement of fruit. Decorate a cake with lighted sparklers. If the event runs into the evening, bring out hurricane lamps and lanterns to light the way indoors and out, to and from the fireworks display.

Casual Parties

The charm of casual entertaining is often the most beguiling. Good thing, too, since for many of us the kind of party we give most often is the nonevent, the "let's-get-together" gathering. We invite a few friends over for supper and poker or bridge. We ask a few people for cocktails. Our best friends or parents join us for Sunday supper. We pack picnics for the afternoon or to take to an open-air concert.

All that is required for the casual party is a desire for company. How about giving a housewarming buffet to celebrate a renovation or to welcome the new neighbors? It could even be potluck—or a Saturday or Sunday lunch. Why not dream a little more and organize a tailgate party for a steeplechase or reunion football game? Or how about breakfast in bed for your spouse? Perhaps you should invite friends from out of town for a weekend.

You need not worry about making things too compli-cated, for casual entertaining should be just that—easy and fuss-free. After all, the point is to have some good company.

Picnics

There is something romantic about the idea of a picnic. Sipping a glass of wine, nibbling lazily on a chicken leg, or daintily downing a little pasta salad, we see ourselves as we most want to be seen: beautiful and relaxed. Somehow there is a universal appeal to eating outside, even if the ants invade, the ground is damp, and we (invariably) forget something.

Picnics provide a terrific chance to use the beautiful picnic basket that seems to be a frequent wedding gift. One couple were given one (their names are painted on the top) over forty years ago and use it to this day. It has had a few repairs over the years, but they wouldn't trade

At a picnic we feel part of a calm and pleasant world, removed from the everyday, when we sip a glass of wine, nibble on a chicken leg, snack on finger foods, or indulge in a rich dessert, such as a lemon tart. CHINA: Carolina CRYSTAL: Atrium

it. They use it for breakfast picnics and lunch on the beach, when it's packed full of sandwich makings, cookies, and fruit.

The children always chuckled at their father's obsessive preparations for a picnic. He made sure the basket was packed with everything needed (but not too much), that the beach umbrella was in the car, the camp stools and beach chairs at hand. Only later did they realize that it was his care that had made their outings seem so easy. They rarely found themselves caught short, yet they traveled light enough that they never had to make more than one trip from the car. One person carried the basket or cooler, another the thermoses, a third the blanket and umbrella, a fourth the chairs.

Some of the father's rituals are useful for us all. He always kept certain basic supplies in the picnic basket. Included were a can and bottle opener, a roll of paper towels, a bag of utensils, salt and pepper shakers, and a stack of plates and cups. These items lived in the picnic basket and only came out when needed.

The family's meals followed a few basic rules, too. They often had sandwiches, but never ones with mayonnaise in the summer unless they came cold from a cooler. They also ate other foods that didn't spoil easily—cheese and chutney sandwiches were big, as were sardine sandwiches and salads made with vinegar-based dressings. They ate ham and chicken, as well as potato salad and coleslaw, but the mother was very careful that they be cold.

When it came to setting the food out, the family had a tablecloth that was used only for picnics. Their children thought there was something quite special about its white background and bold yellow, red, and blue flowers. There were cloth napkins to match, but as the years went on and a few disappeared, they used paper ones. When the mother felt the need for a change in picnic cloths, the favorite was put away.

Now her daughter has taken up the picnic traditions. She packs her own favorite picnic cloth in her own picnic basket, along with the essentials that live there. She takes along today's versions of the foods of her youth. Vegetable and pasta salads often find a place, as do cold chicken and ham sandwiches. Her basket is also packed with pretty but simple plates, silverware, and wineglasses.

Sometimes a simple picnic is transformed into a more substantial affair when you gather with friends at a tailgate picnic (which takes its name from the practice of serving a meal from the extended tailgate of a station wagon). Tailgate picnics are increasingly popular as a way for people to gather and share a meal, often at a

Food on the Go

■

1. *Cool it first. Perishable foods that have been cooked, particularly meats, should be cooled quickly in the refrigerator or freezer before packing in a cooler.*

2. *Beware of mayonnaise spoilage. Dishes containing mayonnaise should be kept cold to prevent spoiling.*

3. *Maintain temperature for texture. Cold mousses and other foods containing gelatin should be kept cold to keep them firm.*

4. *On-site assembly. Sandwiches with moist fillings should be assembled on site to keep them from becoming soggy.*

sporting event such as a steeplechase or football game. While most picnics bring with them a feeling of summer, a tailgate seems to mean fall. You haven't quite given in to the elements and gone inside, but you also aren't spread out on the ground under a tree.

Some people find it a great way to get in the last barbecue of the season by bringing along little hibachis and grilling sliced marinated steak and hamburgers. Thermoses reveal soups and hot apple cider in addition to coffee. Beer and wine are often the mainstay drinks of the day. Brownies, cookies, and cakes make great endings to such a meal, along with crisp fall apples. When each family brings along a contribution, the meal can be a feast indeed.

The rule about keeping things light is not as important when your car plays a central role in the party. Really adventurous tailgaters have been known to bring along folding tables in addition to chairs and barbecues. With such equipment you can set quite a stylish picnic, using a picnic tablecloth, casual china, stainless flatware, real glasses, and cloth napkins. If your garden is brimming with flowers, gather a bunch to take along for a centerpiece.

The Housewarming Buffet

A housewarming just might be the way for you to get to know new neighbors or to show off the hard work you have put into renovating or decorating your home. You don't have to have everything in perfect shape—indeed, it's forgiven, even expected, at such a party that a few boxes or painting tools are still to be found.

One couple had a glorious housewarming after they had renovated their apartment. Almost a year of work had been put into the project, transforming it from a run-down out-of-date apartment into a showplace, complete with a new enlarged kitchen, bright floors, and replastered walls. Their friends had only seen it during its ugly-duckling years and the couple were proud of the finished product. They wanted to show it off, and a housewarming was the obvious choice.

They saw it as a gala event, so they decided to make it a large party, inviting all their friends, both social and business. They also decided to make it a dinner buffet after work. They wondered whether they should serve just wine or have a full bar. Knowing the habits of most of their friends, they decided to have a full selection of drinks available, from soft drinks and juice to wine and cocktails. Since they both work, they also felt it made sense to hire a caterer, complete with a waiter and bartender. At first they thought they would try to use all of their own glassware and china, but quickly realized that they would never have enough. Instead, they rented glasses, cups, and plates but used their own serving pieces.

Next, they decided on a guest list, then on the invitations. Rather than just call people, they wanted to be creative, so they made their own. They worded it very simply, and the woman, an artist, drew clever before-and-after renderings of their apartment. They made photocopies and mailed them about two weeks before the party.

The final preparations were quite easy. The day before the party they did a final cleaning of the apartment. On the day of the party, the woman left work a little early and picked up flowers on the way home. She arranged them in her most beautiful vases while her husband set up the bar area and the buffet table.

Half an hour before the party was to begin the caterer arrived with the food and the waiter and bartender. They helped arrange the food on her platters and they received her instructions about passing hors d'oeuvres to the guests. They also were asked to keep an eye on the table to make sure that the platters stayed full and the table kept clear of litter. Finally, they were instructed to bus plates and glasses as they saw the need, so that people wouldn't be left awkwardly holding their plates and napkins when finished.

When the doorbell rang, the entertainers were relaxed and ready to see their friends, who, of course, were all eager to see them and their beautiful apartment. The rooms soon filled, the talk became animated, and the evening was a success.

The Casual Drop-in Party

Sometimes the best parties happen almost by accident—such as when an old college friend calls up from the airport to say hello. You convince her to come over for supper right then. You hadn't planned on food for an extra person, the house is a mess, and you're getting over a cold, but you just know that you can't let such an opportunity pass. There is no time to worry about it since your friend is on her way.

There are easy ways to make the evening festive. First, set a pretty table. Bring out nice china and a pretty tablecloth or place mats. Set out candles, even if you don't have time to polish the candlesticks. Maybe do a special fold with the napkins.

Making the Most of Potluck
■

The way to get seven different pies and no vegetable dishes or salads is to leave the choice to your guests. Instead, try following these guidelines:

1. *Make up a general menu that includes any contributions that you're sure will arrive.*
2. *Make up a list of additional dishes needed.*
3. *Assign preferred dishes to their creators.*
4. *Offer other dishes, with suggestions if asked, to other participants. Don't offer desserts if you already have an abundance of them and really need salad.*
5. *Be prepared to make necessary dishes yourself to fill in any large holes.*
6. *Have suggestions for nonfood contributions ready for people who don't cook but would like to help out.*

The house doesn't have to be in perfect shape to meet the new neighbors. Just invite people in for an impromptu buffet and make it easy with sandwiches, salad, cheese, and fruit.
CHINA: *Chesapeake* CRYSTAL: *Allure; Optika bowl; Charleston vase*

As for the food, you probably have something in the freezer that could extend the meal. Add another vegetable, or make biscuits or muffins. If you have time, run out and pick up some ice cream to go with fruit and some flowers if the store has them. Your touches will be appreciated as welcome signs when your friend arrives. Even if you don't do a thing, a warm greeting and pleasure in seeing your guest will accomplish the same thing.

Another kind of spontaneous entertaining is that of inviting friends over for a swim, or a drink, or a cup of tea. These invitations are almost always issued by telephone or when you see someone. Such get-togethers need not be elaborate. Perhaps you'll serve just drinks: tea, coffee, cocktails, hot chocolate, or lemonade, and a little something to eat, such as homemade or store-bought cookies, a coffee cake, chips and dip, crudités, or something more elaborate.

All you really need to do is make the party seem effortless and show your guests that they are welcome. One woman makes an unfortunate impression on her guests when she invites her friends over for an afternoon pool party. When she calls her friends to invite them, weeks in advance, she closes each conversation by saying emphatically: "Don't expect a thing to eat—I am only prepared to give you a drink." Her friends hang up the phone wondering if she really wants to see them. The most unfortunate aspect is that the hostess thinks she is being breezy and casual. If only she would say, "Come on over for a swim and a cool drink," and leave out any mention of food, her friends would get the message and go in the spirit she wishes.

Entertaining the Weekend Guest

Entertaining weekend guests can be the most enjoyable kind of visiting as well as the most frustrating and tiring. However, with an easy attitude, a little planning, and the thoughtful selection of guests, it can almost always be rewarding.

Planning certain aspects of the weekend is as much for the host or hostess's peace of mind as it is for the entertainment of the guest, because most people are happy to fall in with whatever happens to be going on. If you follow a few guidelines, you can relax and enjoy your company, secure that their needs are being met.

When planning the weekend, try to determine what your guests particularly like to do. Maybe they like to take walks or shop, attend auctions, sightsee, or sit and talk. Whatever their interests, try to find out in advance and make plans to do one or another of the things they have expressed interest in. If you don't know what they

Welcoming the Weekend Guest

■

Requirements for a good guest bedroom

- *Bed with a firm mattress*
- *Ample pillows, two per person*
- *Adequate lighting for reading in bed*
- *Alarm clock or clock radio*
- *Wastebasket*
- *Ashtrays, if guests smoke*
- *Box of tissues next to the bed*
- *Closet with clothes hangers and space for clothes (preferably an empty closet)*
- *Empty dresser, or at least one empty drawer*

Nice touches for a guest bedroom

- *Vase of fresh flowers*
- *Telephone extension*
- *Calendar, notepaper, and stamps in a desk*
- *Selection of books and magazines*
- *Dark shades or curtains on the windows for guests who like to sleep late*
- *Clothes brush*
- *Pincushion with needles and thread, straight pins, and safety pins*

Requirements for a guest bathroom

- *Fixtures in good order: toilet flushes properly, drains are clear*
- *Plenty of towels: bath, hand, washcloth, bath mat*
- *Fresh bars of soap for bath and basin*
- *Full roll of toilet paper, box of tissues*
- *Good lighting for shaving and applying makeup*
- *Wastebasket*

Nice touches for the bathroom

- *Body and hand lotion, bath powder, bath oil*
- *Aspirin, bandages, antacid*
- *Toothpaste and a new toothbrush*

like, explore various options and have several they can choose from.

You can keep listings of old houses and museums open to the public for the sightseers, the schedule of the local music festival, and the movie listings. A day or two before people arrive, check the local papers to see what's scheduled. Discover the local hiking and walking trails and the hours of the community tennis courts for your energetic friends and the best antiques shops for acquisitive ones.

With all of the possibilities in mind, try not to plan too much, leaving the time and events flexible and allowing a certain amount of independence for everyone. Don't expect everyone to work in the garden with you, but don't exclude them. Don't be afraid to ask guests to help out when you need it. They are almost always happy to pitch in. One of your friends may love to cook more than anything, so when she comes to visit, plan and cook the meals together. Make sure, however, that no one gets stuck doing all the dishes.

The Logistics of Weekend Entertaining

The basic guideline for weekend entertaining is really quite easy to follow—keep it simple. For instance, if your guests arrive on Friday night, plan a simple meal. The commotion of arriving and settling in, not to mention the variables of arrival time, make it difficult to serve an elaborate meal on a tight schedule. Making something that doesn't require exact timing or that can be cooked quickly is a good way to keep the evening meal casual. Serve dinner in the warm atmosphere of candlelight on a table set with pleasing informal china and linens. Over supper you can discuss the possible events of the weekend and make general plans.

When it's time to retire, show guests the ropes. Show them where you keep the coffee and tea and breakfast supplies in case they get up earlier than you do. Also show them where to find the toothpaste and other sundries and the towels, so they can help themselves to as many as they need.

Breakfast the following morning can be fairly simple before setting out on the day's appointed activities. Lunch may be simple again, perhaps a sandwich eaten out. Sometime late in the afternoon find your way home, if the day's activities have been spent out and rest, relax, and prepare for dinner.

Saturday dinner may be more elaborate than the simple Friday supper, for it is this meal that your guests will probably remember as a celebration of the weekend spent together. You need not prepare a particularly fancy meal, but make sure it is carefully thought out and prepared. Sometimes you can make a dish the day before, such as a soup or a marinated meat or chicken dish. Whatever you choose, however, should be fairly easy, since you don't want to spend the whole afternoon in the kitchen when you could be with your guests. In the summer, you can cook meat or fish on the grill; in the winter, broil or roast meats, poultry, or fish. Vegetables need to be prepared simply, since usually there isn't much time, so make sure to use seasonal ones. You can make dessert as elaborate or simple as you wish, using the time before dinner to make a pie or quick cake or relying on ice cream and fresh fruit.

What helps the Saturday evening meal stand out most, however, is the attention you pay to the table. Light lots of candles and try to have flowers or a simple centerpiece. Bring out a slightly more formal tablecloth than you used for the Friday night supper and use cloth napkins. You may want to use more formal china, too, to go along with the slightly elevated tone.

By the time you sit down to dinner, everyone is relaxed and full of talk of the day's events. The evening always passes pleasantly, no one really wanting it to end. After dessert and coffee and plenty of talk, clean up, everyone helping out a little.

Sunday morning you can spend leisurely, although you can also fix a big country breakfast or lunch to keep people going and make it something of a send-off. Eggs scrambled with cheese, fresh herbs, scallions—whatever you find in the refrigerator—often provide the main protein, although you might splurge and broil bacon or kippers. Pancakes with wild blueberries and French toast are also quite popular. People are often astounded when you serve fresh biscuits or muffins—both of which are quite easy to prepare.

When you make a lunch instead of a big breakfast, you can bridge the gap between breakfast and lunch by making a flan or other egg dish and serve bread and a green salad with a simple dressing or a steamed vegetable and a fruit salad.

The table is set informally for breakfast or lunch. Use place mats and informal china and the flowers from the night before to adorn the table. Set the places with a salad or luncheon fork rather than dinner fork. Also set the places with juice glasses and coffee cups for breakfast. People often have coffee at Sunday lunch, so set out cups and saucers, too.

Guests usually leave in the middle of the afternoon, allowing the hosts to luxuriate with the Sunday paper and afternoon naps.

A weekend is a good time to celebrate with a hearty breakfast and a pretty table.
CHINA: *Carolina; Tracery vase* CRYSTAL: *Navarre, Castle Garden*

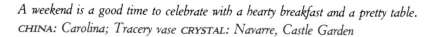

Dessert Party

For people who like to make sweets, the dessert party is the perfect venue for their talents. Such a party also suits the schedules of very busy people or those who don't want to spend an entire evening or afternoon at a party. You set a time—after dinner or in the late afternoon—and invite friends over. You can then serve a selection of your homemade desserts and coffee and tea or dessert wine. You can also make it into a potluck with friends contributing one or two special desserts. You provide a dessert or two and liquid refreshments.

A dessert party can be among the easiest parties to give, since you don't have to plan an entire meal. You should plan the desserts to balance one another, offering a selection of rich, heavy desserts set off by light, fruity ones. For instance, if you serve a mousse, you might also want to have a crisp pastry or firm cake to balance the texture and a fruit salad to balance the richness.

Setting up the desserts on a buffet table is the most sensible method of organizing the food. The table is also adorned with a stack of dessert plates, an arrangement of forks, spoons, and napkins. If you choose to give the party in the evening, you may light the table with candles and decorate it with a bowl or vase of flowers or decorative objects appropriate to the season. If the table still has room, you might use it to serve the coffee and tea.

Sunday Night Supper

Good friends are indeed those you can call on Sunday morning to come over for supper that night. Such a party by its nature is casual and relaxed. The food is usually easy, and so is the service.

In the winter, a warming pot of soup and loaf of bread followed by a simple salad and warm cobbler or pie for dessert make a wonderfully welcoming meal. In the summer, a main-course salad or simple grilled dish, corn on the cob or steamed summer squash, and fresh fruit, such as peaches, nectarines, or slices of watermelon, make an easy and satisfying meal.

A dessert party can be formal or informal, depending on your mood. Here we have a selection of cheese with fruit and elegant desserts. CHINA: *Orleans Blue* CRYSTAL: *Classic Laurel; Optika bowl*

A supper with good friends lends itself to casual serving. You can serve the meal directly from the stove, buffet style in the kitchen, or family style at the dining table.

Serving casually doesn't mean you need to neglect the table. You could use a textured tablecloth or woven place mats, or perhaps you have an attractive quilt or woven bedspread not in use (only recommended if you are serving a relatively neat meal). Bold striped or jacquard design dishcloths and napkins make stunning place mats as well as napkins. Casual or more formal china can look terrific on colorful backgrounds. Light the table with votive candles, dim the lights, and let everyone enjoy the easy companionship of good friends.

Breakfast in Bed

Is there a more romantic notion in the world than breakfast in bed? By definition an intimate party, it can be celebrated anytime you have a lazy morning and an indulgent urge. The meal itself is only a part of the issue, for the pampering is really the key.

Prepare a simple meal, if only so that the event seems spontaneous. Besides, if you keep your recipient waiting too long, he or she might decide it's time to get up. A pair of shirred eggs takes only a few minutes in the oven and a piece of toast just a minute. Add a glass of juice and a cup of coffee or tea to complete the meal. To make it even simpler, make just toast or warm a couple of muffins or brioches. Place them on a plate, add a pat or two of butter and a spoonful of jam, and breakfast is on the way.

The arrangement of the tray itself is of great importance, since it is the conveyer of this romantic meal. You can use any number of items, from a large flat basket to a proper footed breakfast tray complete with pocket for the morning paper. Whatever you use, begin by lining the tray with a napkin (it can be damask, homespun, or lace, —whatever appeals to you in the morning), pretty dish towel, or even a paper doily. Then add the food on an attractive plate, whatever silver is needed, cup and saucer or mug, and juice glass. If there is a pretty blossom at hand, by all means decorate with it, by draping it on the tray or standing it in a bud vase.

If you've chosen a very simple meal, such as muffins and coffee, you can probably fit breakfast for two on the tray. Crawl back into bed yourself to enjoy the luxury.

A warming pot of stew, a loaf of crusty bread, and a group of congenial friends are the makings of a relaxed and casual Sunday night supper.
CHINA: *Chinastone Blue Brushstrokes*
CRYSTAL: *Allure*

Nothing makes a person feel more pampered than waking up to a breakfast tray.
CHINA: *English Rose* CRYSTAL: *Monroe*

Formal Occasions

Formal occasions are the ones we imagine when we think of the rich and famous. The guests are dressed in the finest silks and wear extravagant jewelry; the hosts entertain their visitors in giant marble-floored rooms where armadas of waiters attend to every need and whim.

Such splendid formal occasions do still take place, of course, but formal events are no longer the province of the very rich or the titled. Formal entertaining now is quite the normal thing for people in all walks of life.

It isn't appropriate, of course, for you to don your gown or top hat and tails for just any occasion. On the other hand, some events just cry out for a more structured and elaborate celebration. One thing is sure: there's no reason not to try on a more formal style, just to see if it fits.

Afternoon Tea

The term *afternoon tea* may make you think of drawing room comedies, complete with strolling violins amid potted palms. Or maybe you envision thin bread-and-butter and cucumber sandwiches being consumed by middle-aged matrons in suits and hats while others preside over silver teapots. Whatever comes to mind, afternoon tea in a number of forms is making a well-deserved comeback.

A tea is an excellent way to entertain out-of-town guests or visiting celebrities or to welcome a new friend into your circle. It is also a lovely afternoon alternative to a cocktail party. It provides a good opportunity to entertain formally and stylishly without having to spend a fortune in money or time. Four o'clock is the traditional hour for tea, but anytime between three and six o'clock is appropriate.

Teas by their nature tend to be rather formal, although they can be made as informal as you like. A mug of tea and an oatmeal cookie at your desk doesn't seem special, but put the tea in a thin china cup on a lace cloth and serve it with a few delicate cookies or a slice of cake and you have a party.

A tea menu includes traditional tea dishes, such as a selection of cakes, often cookies or pastries, and small sandwiches. In the old days there was a lot of chicken

More formal entertaining, either business or social, benefits from careful planning and attention to detail.
Here the table is set in advance, requiring only that the candles be lit moments before everyone arrives at
the table. CHINA: *Georgian Shell* CRYSTAL: *Monroe; Charleston salt and pepper set and candlesticks*

salad and ham spread served in crustless little sandwiches. Today's alternatives include sandwiches of sliced smoked chicken or turkey and sliced baked ham served in little rolls or biscuits. Cucumber sandwiches, on the other hand, were, and still are, one of the great treats of a proper tea.

Preparing a tea table is a good opportunity to show off your finest and thinnest china, your most elegant tablecloth, your best silver. This is the event that your silver tea service, should you be lucky enough to have one, was made for.

A proper tea table is set up in the following manner. The tea service, including teapot, water pot, cream pitcher, sugar bowl, and waste bowl is situated on a tray at one end of the table along with a tea strainer and a small plate or bowl of sliced lemon. The other end of the table holds the coffee tray, if coffee is served. This tray holds the coffeepot, cream pitcher, and sugar bowl. The cups and saucers are within easy reach of the person (or persons) who pour.

Small plates, dessert forks, if needed, and napkins matching the tea cloth are arranged on either side of the table. The plates of cake and sandwiches are then arranged attractively in the remaining space. If your table is quite large, or the menu simple, you may have room for an arrangement of flowers or other centerpiece. Candles, however, are not appropriate at teatime unless it gets dark very early. The service is buffet style.

At a small gathering the trea tray is often placed on a low table in the living room or on the dining table. The hostess serves the tea and the food herself, after discovering each guest's preference. At a large tea the hostess usually appoints friends to pour the tea and coffee.

Entertaining the Boss

Some people call it boss-o-phobia, but most of us have felt it. It's the momentary panic that arises when we realize that, having been entertained socially by the boss (yours or your spouse's), you must now return the favor.

Inviting the boss and spouse is not something that you do just for fun, unless yours is an extremely relaxed office. Translating a work relationship to a social one can be very tricky, especially since so many things seem at stake. However, just because the boss comes to dinner does not mean that the rules of behavior change. You act as normally as you can in all respects, maintaining the same essential relationship as in the office.

The Proper Pot of Tea

■

1. *Bring fresh cold water to a boil.*
2. *As soon as the water boils, remove from the heat.*
3. *Warm the teapot by filling it half full of boiling water. Swish it around and pour it out.*
4. *Place a rounded teaspoonful of good-quality loose tea for each cup (teacup, not measuring cup) of water. Pour the boiling water over the leaves to reach half an inch above the leaves.*
5. *Leave to steep for 5 to 10 minutes before adding more boiling water.*
6. *When serving, mix the strong tea with boiling water to accommodate each guest's taste.*
7. *Keep the tea hot.*

NOTE: *When a large quantity of tea must be held for a long time, make the tea on the kitchen stove, actually boiling the leaves for about 3 minutes. Strain the leaves before pouring the tea into the warmed pot. Tea prepared in this manner will not become bitter with sitting—nor will it taste quite as good as freshly brewed.*

Setting a tea table is a matter of balance and accessibility. From these elements you can create a table that is welcoming and easy to use.
CHINA: *English Rose*

The secret, as always, is in the planning. Have as much of the meal ready in advance as possible. Have the house ready, too, and yourself prepared early enough that you can relax briefly before the guests arrive. If you have everything prepared to the best of your ability, you won't have to worry about the mechanics of pulling off a nice evening.

Your duty, as usual, is to act as host or hostess, keeping the party on course by making sure everyone knows one another, has enough food and drink, and has someone to talk with.

Let's walk through such an evening. You've planned a simple but elegant meal that seems in keeping with your status and that shows that you know how to do things right. Your house is neat and clean, and it is obvious that you have taken some care to provide accents for the evening with, say, an attractive arrangement of flowers on the mantelpiece. Your table is set for a formal dinner, as discussed in chapter 8. The settings are again simple but elegant. Everything is under control in the kitchen, needing only last-minute touches before you sit down.

You and your spouse greet each guest at the door, take their coats, and introduce them to one another. You then offer them something to drink. When the boss and his or her spouse arrive, they are treated in exactly the same manner. The boss is addressed as you would do so in the office, and the spouse is addressed in a corresponding manner. If you call your boss Mr. Bigglesworth, then you call his wife Mrs. Bigglesworth, unless they specifically ask you to call them Bill and Barbara.

Excuse yourself a few minutes before dinner is to be served to make the final preparations. Fill the water goblets and set the first course at each place, unless you have help to serve. Whether you choose to serve the plates in the kitchen or *à table*, everything must be on schedule when you sit down. The last thing you do before announcing dinner is light the candles.

When dinner is ready to be served, invite everyone into the dining room. The host will escort the woman guest of honor in to dinner. The other guests follow, the hostess going in last. The hostess directs people where to sit. If the party were for six or ten the seating would be quite simple. The host and hostess would sit at opposite ends of the table, the man of honor would be on the hostess's right and the woman of honor on the host's right, with the guests alternating man and woman. for a table of four couples, however, the seating must work differently. The hostess moves one place to her left, to keep from having two women and two men sitting together, so that the man on her right sits at the end of the table, opposite the host.

At this dinner, the guests sit down to a first course in place. They wait for

Making Introductions

■

Many people feel uncomfortable making introductions and thus often make it more complicated than it need be. There are only a few basic things to remember:

1. *A man is always introduced to a woman. "Mrs. Bigglesworth, I'd like you to meet Peter McFarthing, my colleague."*

2. *A young person is always introduced to an older person. "Miss Minerva, this is my niece Priscilla."*

3. *A less important person is always introduced to a more important one. "Chancellor Hillman, I would like to present Mr. Jones, our neighbor, who is also a geologist."*

4. *Members of your family, female as well as male, are introduced to people out of courtesy.*

5. *Whatever phrases you choose to introduce people, avoid identifying someone as "my friend," as it implies that the person you are addressing is not.*

6. *Try to include a phrase to identify the people being introduced. This will give them a conversational opening.*

everyone to be seated before eating and do so only when the hostess gives a signal, saying, for example, "Please begin." The first course plates are removed before the rest of the meal is served. At our small dinner, the host will serve the meal, since he is carving a leg of lamb. Were it a different meal, the plates might be assembled in the kitchen and placed before each guest. In any case, he serves the lady of honor on his right first. The next plate is passed down the right side to the person seated opposite him. The remaining guests on the right side are then served, working back toward the guest of honor. The procedure is repeated on the left side. After three or four people have been served, the hostess urges her guests to begin eating, as the food will become cold.

Unless there is a hired person to help, the hostess or host usually clears the table and all offers of help from guests are refused. When clearing, plates are removed two at a time—never stacked. It may take longer, but it is more pleasant.

On your way back to the dining room, you may bring in the plates for the next course and either place them in front of the guests or on a sideboard. Once the salad course has been served, all dishes are cleared from the table, including condiments such as salt and pepper, since they couldn't possibly be used for dessert. Dessert may be served from the kitchen or by the hostess or host. You need not clear the dessert dishes from the table until after your guests leave.

Coffee is served after or with dessert either at the table or in the living room, and the thoughtful host or hostess offers both decaffeinated and regular. Liqueurs are often served from a tray after coffee. Guests may indicate their pleasure to the host or pour their own. (See chapter 8 for a discussion of courses and settings.)

You will end the evening back in the living room either with a cup of after-dinner coffee, or a liqueur, or both, in pleasant conversation. At an appropriate hour, Mr. and Mrs. Bigglesworth or one of the other guests will make motions to leave. They will say nice things about the evening and you will respond in kind, mentioning how happy you are that they were able to come.

Dining at the White House: The Ultimate Honor

It certainly doesn't happen to everyone, but someday you might find yourself invited to dine at the most important home in the country, the White House. If entertaining the boss makes you nervous, imagine what dining out at 1600 Pennsylvania Avenue will do. Even if you never dine with the President, you may well find yourself faced with attending a very formal dinner. Whichever you find yourself invited to, protocol prescribes so much for you that it will be easier than you think.

To begin with, you will receive a formal invitation. Of course, you accept the invitation immediately upon receipt with a formal written response (see chapter 2). There are very few reasons for not accepting a White House invitation, but they include illness, unbridgeable geographical distance, and a marriage or death in the family. Should you need to decline the invitation, the wording of the response is essentially the same as for any formal note of regret, except that you must briefly mention the reason you cannot attend. This is how it would look:

Mr. and Mrs. Samuel Butler
regret extremely that owing to the illness
of Mr. Butler
they will be unable to accept
the kind invitation of
The President and Mrs. Jefferson
to dinner
on Tuesday, the twenty-ninth of July

An invitation to the White House will also include an admittance card that must be shown on your arrival. Don't lose it; you might not get in without it.

Next, plan your attire. Men wear black tie to dinner at the White House (and most formal dinners), unless the invitation states otherwise, and women wear conservative, long evening dresses. This is not the time to go Hollywood with a low-neckline or off-the-shoulder dress with a skirt slit to the thigh, since dinner at the White House is to be regarded as essentially a business dinner. For a very formal social dinner you may please yourself in the choice of your evening gown.

The day arrives, after weeks of telling your friends of your good fortune. You set out in good time for your appointed arrival. In fact, you will need to arrive a few minutes early, because the President and First Lady will arrive at the stated hour and you must be there before they appear. For any formal occasion you should arrive within a few minutes of the stated time.

You find yourself at the gate of the White House, admittance card in hand. The Secret Service checks it and you are ushered in. After you remove your coat, you will be shown in to the room where you will be received along with the other guests.

At the appointed hour, the President and First Lady arrive. If the group is small, they will walk around the room greeting the guests. If the party is large, they will stand and receive them. When passing through the receiving line, the person of the most official prominence precedes his or her spouse. If the wife is the Cabinet officer or Senator, she precedes her husband, and vice versa. (In most formal receiving lines the wife always goes first.) You greet the President and First Lady by saying, "Good evening." You don't engage in conversation unless the President initiates it. If he does, you call him "Mr. President" and "Sir" and his wife by her proper name, "Mrs. Jefferson."

Once through the receiving line you may find yourself mingling with the other guests. When you do, stick to pleasantries, particularly when speaking with someone you don't know and are not likely to meet at any other time. If you try to ask about the Secretary's position on foreign affairs, most likely you will be met with comments on the weather, the dinner, and the after-dinner entertainment.

When you find yourself mingling with the other guests, it is always proper to introduce yourself and your spouse if there is no one else to do it. You refer to yourselves by your names and, if you wish, can mention how you happen to be there. The people you meet will do the same.

If someone else introduces you, it's quite easy to know what to call your fellow guests. Generally you call people by title. For instance, if someone introduces you to Representative Patricia Schroeder and her husband by saying, "Representative Patricia Schroeder and Mr. James Schroeder, I would like you to meet Mr. and Mrs. John Jones," you will thereafter call the Representative by her title, Representative Schroeder, and her husband by his name, Mr. Schroeder. The same is true of others with such titles. When introduced to a Supreme Court justice, you would call him or her by title and last name, such as Justice O'Connor. An ambassador would be referred to as Ambassador Gillard and his wife as Mrs. Gillard. If a Cabinet member is introduced to you as "The Secretary of the Interior, Mr. Hawkings," call him or her by the title Mr. Secretary or Madame Secretary.

It helps, of course, if you know the names and titles of prominent officials so that you don't find yourself uttering the words, "And what do you do for the government?" only to find that you are speaking to the Secretary of Labor.

Once dinner has been announced, the President will go into the dining room first with the highest-ranking woman guest. At any dinner the host leads the guests with the woman of honor or highest-ranking woman guest. The First Lady follows with the highest-ranking man. At other formal parties, the hostess remains behind and follows her guests in. Remaining guests at the White House will then be ushered in to the dining room, where you will find your place indicated by your place card. Place cards go by title or name. The President's reads, "Mr. President." Cabinet members are listed as, for example, "The Secretary of Labor," Ambassadors as, for example, "The Ambassador of France." Mere mortals know themselves by their names: "Mrs. John Jones."

Once you find your place, you may sit down if you are a lady, while gentlemen seat the ladies on their right before sitting themselves. Before you will be a formal place setting. When you sit you unfold your napkin, place it on your lap, and wait to be served. When served you may begin, unless the party is quite small, when you see the First Lady begin. As with all place settings, use the outside implements first and work in for each course (see chapter 8).

Once the meal is under way, go with the flow. The staff will serve you, so you needn't worry about portion sizes or anything like that. If wine goes to your head easily, drink sparingly, for this is the last place you want to feel the least bit out of control. If presented with a small bowl of water at the end of the meal, dip the tips of your fingers in it lightly, tapping them on your napkin. None of this is as formidable as you might think, since the White House staff is well trained in gently leading people through each step of the meal.

As far as your dinner partners go, make sure to speak with the people on either side of you. Depending on the table size and shape, it may be easy to speak with other guests as well. Once again, stick to general conversational topics.

After dinner there will probably be entertainment. If you notice more people after dinner, this is probably because some people are invited for the entertainment alone. After-dinner entertainment may include anything from a musical performance by a noted pianist to a dance band playing current favorites, at which everyone joins in. Unless you are a powerful person or a good friend of the President and First Lady, don't ask the First Lady to dance. This is a social evening, but not casual.

There is an old rule that says that no one may leave the party before the President retires. Generally speaking, the President and First Lady will retire fairly early to give everyone a chance to get home at a decent time, and you are free to leave after they do. However, certain presidents have been known to dance the evening away, and you are not required to stay. At other formal parties, the traditional rule required that everyone stay until the guest of honor left, but this has been relaxed and you are free to go when it seems appropriate.

Part Three

TECHNIQUES
OF TABLECRAFT

Setting the Table

Eating is a pleasure and the experience is to be savored. Part of its pleasure comes from the ritual of the table. A crucial element to any meal—whether it's tea for two or a feast for two hundred—is the table and its setting. The dishes and utensils and the glassware must be chosen with care, in the same way that we choose the meal, the wine, and our guests. Setting a table attractively, whether it be a rough oak table with the bare essentials or a polished antique gleaming with white linen and old silver, shows how much we care about pleasing our guests.

Table settings are compositions, too, providing beautiful design as well as the equipment needed for the meal. By understanding the basic vocabulary of table setting—not only the name, but the purpose and role of each element—you can become an accomplished stylist. It's all part of being able to make guests feel welcomed, dazzled, and cosseted.

Organizing Seating Arrangements

Positioning your guests at the dinner table requires a psychologist's eye for personality and a chemist's instinct for combinations. It's a thoughtful task the hostess or host performs in order for guests to enjoy one another's company. At its simplest, the idea is to provide your guests with entertaining companions, perhaps with loquacious people placed near people who are good listeners, shy people near outgoing people, old friends near new acquaintances. Another reason for organizing seating is so you avoid that embarrassing moment when guests are milling about the dining table waiting for you to exert your authority and find yourself at a momentary loss as to where to put everybody.

Some people regard such planning as fussy and old-fashioned, preferring to leave their guests to sort out their

The great variety of table linens available, such as the selections of damask shown here,
help create or accentuate the mood of any party.

111

seating themselves. The random they'll-figure-it-out approach is fine for a small group of close friends, but rather shortsighted for large gatherings. Surely everyone has been to a party at which one or two tables seemed to have all the sparkling people, while the others were filled with shy people who had nothing in common. You noticed it all the more when you were at the less-than-fortunate tables, enviously watching or listening to the gaiety nearby.

Such discomfort can be avoided with simple planning. At informal, small gatherings seating is quite simple. Alternate men and women as much as possible, keeping spouses separated. They see each other all the time and should have a chance to speak with others.

Seating for larger parties requires a little more thought. Take a guest list and mentally divide it by characteristics. First, if you know that certain guests would enjoy one another, place them together. Avoid, however, playing favorites and creating whole tables that work beautifully, leaving others as ill-sorted collections.

Sunday night supper with close friends is a relaxed time. CHINA: *Chinastone Blue Brushstrokes* CRYSTAL: *Allure*

Talkers should be placed near listeners so that both can benefit. People with similar interests should generally be placed near one another. However, if you have a table of ten and eight of them share the same enthusiasm, excluding the other two, rearrrange the seating to create more of a mix. Similarly, a table with a few people who work in the same office can be fine, so long as the others don't find themselves bored by office gossip and confused by work jargon.

People with similar political views often enjoy discussing their interests, but here again, mix it up a little. It's tedious listening to people agreeing with another about all the same issues; a little controversy can keep things lively. But take care that the potential debaters are the sort who can argue for fun. People who take controversy too seriously may become upset and cause discomfort to others. They might better be seated with people more likely to discuss a wide range of topics on a less intense level.

If the party is a large family event, try to sprinkle family members around. There should be at least one family member or very close friend who can serve as head at every table. This person should act as host, making sure everyone has what they need and trying to keep the conversation interesting. This way everyone feels a part of the action. Once the general seating arrangement is planned, you can begin thinking about the table and how it will look.

Dressing the Table

Tablecloths

Before you can begin setting the table, you must make some decisions about what goes underneath the china and glassware. Tablecloths, place mats, and runners serve the practical purpose of protecting the table, but then there is an element of style involved, too. Anyone who has ever set a table has seen how linens, almost as much as the china and crystal, set the mood of the table and room.

A tablecloth provides the overall canvas on which the composition of place settings, centerpiece, and serving pieces is made. Nothing looks as crisp, formal, and elegant as a starched white damask tablecloth or as delicate as a lace cloth over a light-colored undercloth or dark bare table. A homespun checked cloth welcomes the casual guest and a brightly colored or large-flowered cloth amuses. Tablecloths come in every conceivable pattern, ranging from bright to soft colors, bold to demure flowers, broad stripes to pinstripes, plaids to checks. They may cover the table completely or be draped at an angle. They can reach to the floor or barely over the edge. They can even define a table space on the ground or tailgate of a car.

A formal dinner table is traditionally draped with a conservative white linen damask cloth. It is usually placed over a table pad or blanket that serves to soften sound and keep the cloth in place. A pad also protects a valuable table. Linen cloths are suitable in any decorating scheme. These days, however, you don't have to be so limited. A color that picks up those of the china, flowers, or room decor can work well. Lace and cotton tablecloths are also used, often over a bare table.

What about the creases that appear in folded linens? They are perfectly acceptable, for it is silly to have to iron a cloth each time you use it. However, if your cloth does have creases, they should run absolutely straight on the table.

People also wonder about the length of the cloth. At formal dinners, and most seated dinners for that matter, the cloth should hang about eighteen inches from the edge of the table. Such a length allows the cloth to fall gracefully yet not hamper the legs of the diners. Luncheon cloths don't usually overhang the table by more than a few inches. Buffet cloths, on the other hand, often fall to the floor.

Whether your linens are family heirlooms or brand new from the shop, a beautiful table often begins with the cloth.

You have much more latitude when setting the table for informal entertaining, choosing bright colors, bold patterns, or interesting textures in both cloths and place mats. Picnics and barbecues outside really bring out imaginative qualities, since in addition to informal picnic cloths some people use bedspreads, quilts, and even colorful sheets.

Place Mats

Place mats show off a beautiful table better than almost anything, while still affording protection. As everyone knows, they come in a variety of styles, fabrics, and textures. People use them most frequently for informal dinners, suppers, breakfasts, and lunches.

Formal linen and cutwork place mats, traditionally used for luncheons with a runner, are now more frequently seen at informal dinners. Place mats are never used at very formal dinners, as they are deemed too casual. Beautiful lace and linen place mats are the preferred covering at formal luncheons, however. For more informal dinners and lunches you can use any kind of place mat, from handwoven Indian cotton to straw—even pretty starched dish towels.

The completely bare table set with china and crystal is yet another option for the informal meal. (In this context, *informal* means anything but the absolute most formal of dinners.) Indeed, the high table at Trinity College, Cambridge University, one of the most elegant and prestigious of dining halls, is set every night with beautiful old silver, white damask napkins, silver candelabra, crystal wineglasses, and white china on bare scrubbed oak tables. Nothing could be more formal than the dons proceeding into the room, dressed in academic gowns, the head of college reciting a Latin prayer before anyone sits under the watchful eye of Holbein's portrait of Henry VIII.

Napkins

The next decorative item is the indispensable napkin. You can do without tablecloths and place mats but not without napkins. Here again, almost anything can do as a napkin, from the most formal of white damask to a crisp dish towel, not to mention pretty paper napkins.

The formal dinner napkin, the most luxurious of napery, is a twenty-four-inch square of linen damask. It is white and often monogrammed in one corner. It is folded in one of two ways. The first is to make a rectangular package by folding the square in half, then quarters to make a smaller square, which is, in turn, folded once more to form a rectangle, the thick fold facing to the right. The other method is to fold the napkin into the smaller square as above, then on the diagonal to form a right triangle. Then, folding on the longest side, fold the two ends to the back, dividing the napkin into thirds. Once folded, the formal dinner napkin may then be placed on the service plate or to the left of the forks, but never under the forks. A formal dinner napkin is also used for buffets, when people will be eating off their laps and thus need a nice big area of protection.

Most dinner napkins run a good deal shy of the size of a truly formal napkin, ranging from about sixteen to twenty inches square. They may be used for all kinds of meals, including fairly formal dinners. Colored napkins can help decorate a table by setting off the china, tablecloth, flowers, or other decorations. Napkins may also be folded in a variety of ways, both fanciful and practical. Fancy shapes add interest to settings, showing that the hostess took time over the table. They are placed in the center of the place setting or to the left of the forks, as are formal napkins.

The luncheon napkin, often colored, is smaller than the average dinner napkin at roughly twelve inches square. It is generally folded simply, as is the formal napkin, since it is too small for most fancy folds and is placed in the center of the setting, usually on the luncheon plate. Luncheon-sized napkins may be used for more than luncheons, being a particularly nice size for breakfasts, teas, and picnics.

The little cocktail napkin is most often seen in paper these days, cradling a cold drink. It is helpful as a coaster or receptacle for toothpicks, olive pits, and paper wrappers. Cloth cocktail napkins, seldom seen but very pretty and elegant, can be quite a stylish as well as useful adornment to an icy highball glass or wine goblet. One advantage to cloth napkins is that they don't shred when wet with condensation from a glass.

Choosing Place Settings

Proper place settings are determined by the kind of party being given. Consisting of dishes, cutlery, and glassware required for the courses to be served, settings range from the most elaborate for very formal dinners to the simplest for a casual gathering of close friends for supper. It is as simple as that.

The first decision to be made is which china to use. This is very easy for most of us, since we usually have one or two basic sets of informal and formal china, and the kind of party usually determines which is appropriate. Obviously, Sunday night supper with intimate friends could call for the everyday china, while dinner with the boss calls for your very best. You should be aware, however, that your best china looks great with any meal and you will want to enjoy using it often.

As for flatware, sterling silver is appropriate for any meal, although stainless is perfectly acceptable for most forms of casual entertaining. The designs in both silver and stainless are wide enough to cover almost every need. Some people choose to have a sleek modern stainless and a more traditional sterling pattern.

Glassware follows much the same form. Beautiful stemware is much the same as sterling in that it always looks elegant, whether it is of the finest quality or merely functional. The size of the glass is most important, and for most meals you can use an all-purpose wineglass, unless you will be serving more than one kind of wine.

Many people find the notion of table settings confusing and intimidating. As in many things in life, it's a good deal easier in practice than it seems at first glance. It may help to keep in mind that there is no single correct way to set a table, just as there is no one meal to serve.

The overall goal is always the same: to set a pleasing and functional table. To begin, that means the table should be set so that the elements balance one another. Settings should be equal distances apart, with one foot or two feet between them, preferably, to allow each diner space to maneuver.

A very informal place setting with which most of us are familiar. From the left: salad fork (indicating the salad is to be served as a first course), dinner fork, dinner plate, dinner knife, and teaspoon.

There are a number of ways to be more formal while retaining a certain technical informality. Here the place is set for a three-course dinner. The main setting from the left goes this way: dinner fork, salad fork, dinner plate with napkin in place, salad knife, and dinner knife. Above the main setting appear, from the left: bread-and-butter plate with butter knife, dessert fork and spoon with place card beneath, water goblet, and wineglass.

This informal dinner setting shows the main course. From the left: salad plate, dinner fork, salad fork, dinner plate, salad knife, dinner knife; above the setting from the left: bread-and-butter plate with butter knife, place card, water goblet, and wineglass.

Here's another simple main-course setting for an informal dinner. From the left: dinner fork, salad fork, dinner plate, salad knife, dinner knife. Above the setting are water goblet and wineglass.

This setting for an informal dinner shows the salad course served after the main course. It includes, from the left: salad fork, salad plate, salad knife. Above the setting, from the left: bread-and-butter plate with butter knife, place card, water goblet, and wineglass. The dessert service will be brought in separately.

This setting represents one approach to serving the dessert course at an informal meal. The dessert service is brought in after the previous course has been cleared. The dessert fork and spoon arrive on the plate, and the diner places the fork and spoon on the tablecloth. The coffee cup arrives with spoon on the saucer. (At a formal dinner coffee would be served after dessert had been cleared rather than with the final course.)

A formal place setting need not be intimidating. It's essentially an informal setting without a bread-and-butter plate and sometimes with a few more utensils.

This setting is for a five-course meal: soup, fish, entree, salad, and dessert. From the left: fish, dinner, and salad forks; service plate with napkin; salad, dinner, and fish knives; soup spoon. Above the plate from left to right: place card; water goblet; white wineglass, sherry glass, red wineglass.

This setting shows the layout of the four-course formal meal with the soup plate in place. The soup bowl rests on the service plate, and both will be removed once the course is finished to be replaced by a dinner plate. From the left: dinner fork, salad fork, service plate holding soup plate, salad knife, dinner knife, soup spoon.

A formal setting at the entree course. From the left: dinner fork, salad fork, dinner plate, salad knife, dinner knife; water goblet; red and white wine glasses.

When setting the table for an elaborate multicourse meal, there is one key rule to follow: no more than three of any one kind of utensil appear in a setting. To have more than three forks or three knives in a setting is confusing. Should you be serving a seven-course meal, utensils for additional courses are to be brought in with each course.

Keep in mind as you select your settings that each piece in a table setting should be used. Then position the elements in order of use within a basic rectangular shape, the plate forming the center of the setting. The silver is arranged in the order in which the pieces will be used, with the diners moving from the outside in. The glassware is placed above the silver on the right, since most people are right-handed and can thus lift a glass without reaching over the food. The bread-and-butter plate, if any, is placed above the setting on the left. These are the ground rules; different kinds of service have their own needs.

Casual Settings

The setting that most of us are familiar with is the very informal casual dinner setting. This is the simplest of settings, since it is confined usually to two or three courses. A setting for a two-course meal includes (left to right): dinner fork, salad fork, napkin, plate, dinner knife, and teaspoon. If the main course is to be passed rather than served by the head of the table, the dinner plate would be in the center of the setting, and the napkin to the left of the forks.

If salad is served before the main course (making it a three-course meal), you might find a salad fork to the left of the dinner fork. You also might find a salad bowl or plate slightly above and to the left of the forks. Salad is sometimes served directly on the dinner plate, in which case the dinner fork is used. The teaspoon is used for dessert, although you can also use a salad or dessert fork. Water glass and wineglass, if used, are placed above the knife. A small plate of butter often appears on the table with its own butter knife. A salt and pepper set for the table usually appears also.

Informal Dinners

An informal dinner, which can cover a wide diversity of dinners, including some that are relatively formal, usually involves a number of courses. In days past, when people had lots of help in the kitchen and at table and when people had prodigious appetites, they often served more than half a dozen courses. Today things are simpler, and four or five courses are standard.

A four-course dinner begins with a first course of soup or other dish and continues through entree, salad, and dessert. A five-course meal begins with an appetizer before the first course or includes a fish course after the first course and before the entree.

If soup is the first course, the setting would be (left to right): dinner fork, salad fork, napkin or service plate, salad knife (if used), dinner knife, and soup spoon. If shellfish is the first course, an oyster fork would take the place of the soup spoon and would be placed either to the left of the dinner fork, or in place of the soup spoon. If fish is the first course, you would place a fish fork and knife to the left and right, respectively, of the dinner fork and knife. If salad is served as a first course, the salad fork and knife, if used, would take the outside position.

Around the basic setting a number of other elements are arranged. To the left of the forks you might have a salad plate, or it might be brought in after the entree has been cleared. Above the forks you will find a bread-and-butter plate, usually with a small butter knife placed on it horizontally, vertically, or at an angle, with the handle facing toward the glasses. Butter may be placed on the plate or served on one or two plates for the table. Directly above the plate you might find a place card. The place card also might be positioned on the napkin or service plate, if one is used. Centered above the plate and slightly above the bread-and-butter plate you might find the dessert fork and spoon, placed horizontally, the fork tines facing right, the spoon above it, with the bowl facing left. Alternatively, the dessert service may be brought in after the salad has been cleared. A dessert fork may also appear to the right of the dinner fork.

Finally we reach the glasses. Glasses are placed above the knives. The water is on the left and the wineglasses, white, red, and champagne or sherry (rarely seen, and only when soup is the first course), arrayed to its right either in a line or grouped so they they are easy to reach, as the space allows.

Depending on how formal the meal is and for a large number of people, the table may also be set with individual salt and pepper sets, or one to two sets for the table.

When a guest is seated, the center of the setting will include either a napkin holding the place, or a service plate holding the napkin or the first course. If the first course is in place, the napkin appears to the left of the forks, not under them, since the setting would be disturbed by extricating the napkin.

In any case, the first-course plate or bowl rests in the center of the setting or on the service plate, if used. The service plate is in a pattern different from the main china service. It is commonly a fine china plate, often highly decorated, slightly larger than the dinner plate, but it can also be a dinner plate from another service. Should the first course be served in a stemmed glass, a luncheon-sized plate may serve as the service plate or be used on top of the service plate.

Once the first course has been finished, both the service plate and the first-course plate or bowl are removed, to be replaced by the dinner plate. (All courses, by the way, are served or passed from the left and cleared from the right.)

After the guests finish the entree, the plate is cleared and replaced by the salad plate. Once the salad has been finished, its plate is cleared to make way for dessert. The dessert service may appear with the fork and spoon on the plate. When this is the case, the diner takes them and places them on the table on either side of the plate as a small standard setting. Coffee cups and saucers with spoons may also be brought in at this time and served with dessert. The coffee may be served at the table or from the kitchen. Coffee may also be served after dessert.

You might also find a finger bowl on a doily (which is optional) and small plate resting on the dessert plate. If so, the diner places the finger bowl and its doily and small plate above and to the left of the setting.

The Formal Setting

Most of us have little chance to use the formal setting, since it is seen only at the most formal of occasions, such as state dinners, on cruise ships, and those at which there is plenty of staff to serve. Contrary to what most of us think, it is usually a little simpler than the elaborate informal settings.

The rules for setting are, however, just a little more rigid. To begin, the formal table is always set symmetrically (a good idea in general, since symmetry is always pleasing to the eye). Place settings are evenly spaced with plenty of room between places. The centerpiece is where its name implies. All other decorations, such as candles, place cards, menu cards, and flowers, are arranged with an eye to maintaining a visual balance.

When the diner sits, the elements appear almost identical to the informal setting, with a few notable exceptions. First, there is no bread-and-butter plate with knife, for they are not used. Each setting or two has a salt and pepper set, often placed where the bread-and-butter plate would be.

A service plate always holds the place in a formal setting. The napkin never rests on the service plate, but rests to the left of the forks. Rarely is the first course in place when guests are seated. Instead, it is brought in and placed on the service plate. Salad is also never served before the entree, so the salad fork is always to the right of the dinner fork. A salad plate does not appear as part of the setting.

Dessert is handled in one manner. The service is brought in after the entree has been cleared as described in the informal setting. Coffee is served after dessert, often in another room.

Buffets

There are two basic options for place settings for meals served buffet fashion. When guests will be seated at tables, their places are set as for an informal dinner, using the appropriate utensils for the individual courses. When guests will be finding perches for themselves here and there, the silverware is presented at the end of the buffet table, either rolled in a napkin or arranged for the diners to pick up each piece separately.

Buffet plates are slightly larger than dinner plates to accommodate the moveable aspect of the dinner. They may help cut down on spilling. Use them if you have them, but they are not really necessary. Service plates may be used for buffets as well, but dinner plates are most often used.

The focus of the buffet table itself is the food and necessary utensils. If there is room, add a flower arrangement and a set of candles. However, it is better to forgo the extras in favor of the necessities. Get the food and utensils located first, then worry about decorations. Plates, silverware, and napkins should be available to guests either on the main table or next to it on a smaller table.

The way you arrange the food depends on what you want to feature. One logical method is to start with the entrees and follow it with vegetables and bread. If you are serving a rich entree that calls for small servings, you might put the breads and vegetables in advance of the entree, in the hope that your guests will see their plates fill up before they reach the main course. The best way to control portions is to have someone serve the entree.

If your primary object in setting the table is beauty, consider arranging the dishes in a manner that shows them off to their best advantage, playing off the colors and textures of the various dishes. If you have a large group of people, split the table, mirroring the dishes, and have guests serve themselves from either side. However you choose to arrange dishes, try to leave ample space between bowls or platters so that guests may rest their plates on the table while serving themselves.

Decorating the Table

Centerpieces

While the place setting is the basis of the table, there are other elements that help to create the whole. The most eye-catching and important of these is the centerpiece.

Many of us think instinctively of flowers to decorate a table. Everyone responds to the beauty of fresh flowers, and they can coordinate well with china and linens. The options are limitless, given the endless varieties of sizes, shapes, colors, and textures available. You can find a bloom to go with virtually anything.

When selecting flowers, consider their height, shape, and color. Low bowls of flowers focus the eye on the table and its settings. Tall vases of flowers add a dramatic effect to a table, but shouldn't be so tall that they interfere with guests' vision of one another. The centerpiece for a buffet table, however, can be of any height you wish —the more dramatic the better—since people don't usually need to see around it. Another consideration to keep in mind is that powerfully scented flowers can easily compete with the delicate aromas of food, sometimes creating a muddle of aromas, so try to keep the fragrance of the bouquet subtle.

While flowers are always lovely for centerpieces, there are many other choices, both practical and beautiful. Crystal bowls or baskets of luscious ripe fruit always suit an informal breakfast or lunch table. Cornucopia arrangements of seasonal vegetables and nuts are appropriate as accents to autumn entertaining.

Beautiful decorative objects make wonderful centerpieces, too. Some people have lovely old tureens, decorated bowls, or figurines in china and glass. People with a good eye for visual combinations can take diverse objects and put them together, sometimes to surprising advantage. One hostess has a large collection of stone eggs. She often arranges some of them in a glass bowl to make a most effective centerpiece.

A floral centerpiece graces the buffet. CRYSTAL: *Classic Laurel*

It looks accidental, but the eggs balance one another in color and shape, perched in a simple but effective design.

Almost anything can be used as a centerpiece, but several things should be kept in mind when creating one. Once again, make sure that it is low enough so people can see each other across the table. Craning one's neck to see another guest both discourages conversation and is tiring. Never use artificial flowers, for they always undermine the time and effort you invest in the rest of the table. They make it look as if you took the easy way out. If you want a permanent centerpiece, consider using good quality crystal flowers and fruit.

Lighting

For many of us, candles are essential to a dinner party. They provide a warm, welcoming light that implies friendship or intimacy. A room lit with candles has mystery and beauty. Candlelight makes everyone look softer, and people respond to it with a smile. Conversation becomes more active in candlelight, and the guests see one another with increased interest.

These days such a variety of candle styles and colors are available that they can be a help in coordinating the decoration of the table. We can light a whole room with dozens of candles for one effect, run a line of votive candles down a table for another. A single taper can be used to highlight a specific spot.

There are two considerations in selecting candles. First, table candles should be free of scent (as with the flowers, one doesn't want other smells to fight with the aroma of the food). Second, they should be either high enough or low enough that diners are not blinded by them when looking across the table at their fellow guests.

As a general rule, one candle per person will provide enough light if there is no other illumination and the room is not especially large. If you have another light source, a pair of candles on a table for four or six is adequate. You can always use more, of course.

As is the case with most everything else at a formal dinner party, there are rules about using candles. First, they must be white in order to conform with the linens. White is the most useful color anyway, since it goes with just about every kind of china and linen. Second, you must use new candles. Candles with drips or of differing heights just don't look neat and crisp. Third, they are lighted before the guests enter the dining room. That way guests see the room at its best.

The candles are left lighted until the guests leave the room, so people won't feel as though the party is ending and they are part of the cleaning up. The only exception is when the candles have burned down completely and the guests are still having a great time at the table. Then they may be extinguished with regret.

Using Place Cards

Place cards are a great invention for parties of more than eight people. Their purpose, of course, is to show guests where to sit, and even very simple ones can also lend style to a well-set table.

The traditional place card is white, about $3\frac{1}{2} \times 2$ inches unfolded. It can be colored or decorated in any imaginable way—for example, adorned with a bit of ribbon and lace with tiny dried flowers. For informal parties, you can make place cards using any heavy paper or card stock, using colors or patterns to coordinate with the table scheme.

The guest's name is written on the card as, for example, "Mr. John Johnson, Jr.," if formal, or "John," if informal. If you have a beautiful calligraphic hand, you can make flowing and elegant place cards. If your handwriting is illegible, use a typewriter, since the important thing about the writing is that it be clear.

A Few Final Touches

A party provides the perfect opportunity to entertain guests with little surprises. There is something both charming and complimentary about sitting down and finding a small wrapped box or party favor at your place at the table. Such favors may vary widely, but have been known to include Christmas crackers, personal tokens of affection, dimestore jokes, tiny baskets of nuts or candy, or sprigs of flowers. Whatever is used, it is almost guaranteed to please any guest and win you notices as a thoughtful host or hostess.

Another very nice touch for formal dinners is an individual menu for each guest, preferably written in a beautiful calligraphic script. It is placed on the service plate or to the left of it, either flat or rolled and tied with a little ribbon. Often a menu for every two people is placed between place settings. Sometimes a single menu propped on a ceramic menu stand written on a heavy card is placed for everyone to see—it's not a keepsake, but an advance hint of the culinary pleasures to come.

Other decorative elements can provide your table with a personal touch. The most common and easiest is to fold napkins in a fancy way. Another is to run ribbons and streamers down the length of a festive table. Still another is to decorate individual

A small personal gift, a lavender sachet, a Serenade fragrance bottle, and a miniature ceramic swan all make thoughtful party favors and lovely table decorations.

settings with flowers and fruit or decorative objects from your own collection.

One woman with a flair for decoration has a large collection of wooden and ceramic rabbits (her birthday, which is in the early spring, has for decades been the occasion on which her family and friends contribute to her substantial stable of them). Whenever she entertains in the spring, she creates charming groupings of her bunnies. Rabbit bands march down the table, and small groupings of attentive rabbits appear to watch. Sometimes parts of her collection appear on occasional tables or are massed imaginatively on her mantelpiece.

Holidays and birthdays are the obvious times for letting the frivolity within us all take charge, even if only for a moment. Few of us really outgrow a love of birthday parties complete with balloons, blowers, and party hats. Indulge yourself and your guests, and invest some of the spirit of the day in the way you make your table speak to your guests. Even within the guidelines for properly setting your table, there's ample room for expressing your delight at the occasion—and at the fact that your friends have honored you with their presence.

Choosing and Caring for Tableware

When we're first on our own, most of us start out with dishes that are merely serviceable. The first apartment or home-away-from-home is full of hand-me-downs, including the china.

For many of us, the first opportunity to choose lasting china comes when we decide to marry. For others it is when we have reached a certain professional status and begin to have a little extra money to spend on ourselves and our furnishings. We go to the stores, often with a loved one, we look at hundreds of patterns, and simply can't decide. "How do I know what I'll need or like in ten years?" we ask ourselves. There are ways to think it through.

Choosing China

The first consideration when choosing china is to find patterns that you like. Of course, cost is often an issue, but it should not be the overriding one. Instead, you need to think in terms of your needs now and in the future, and to look for good quality and pleasing designs. After all, consider how often you will be using your china—every day. Whether you choose stoneware or fine china, good-quality china lasts longer and sets a more attractive table.

If you choose wisely, your first pattern may be compatible with later patterns and thus be usable in tandem, as you collect enough of your better china to use alone.

The ideal way to buy china is to buy two compatible patterns, one for casual use and one for more formal entertaining. By choosing both a formal and casual service, you will be preparing for the future. Choose a pattern that you can afford now and a fine china pattern that you can add to for years to come. You may be able to afford a good deal of the everyday pattern now, or people might give it as a present if you are getting married. The more formal or expensive set may be one that you add to gradually, or when generous people give it as a gift.

Plates stacked and ready for buffet service or table setting. CHINA: *Eclipse*

Kinds of China

At its most basic, china is clay that has been formed into vessels and fired. Varieties include earthenware, stoneware, fine china, and bone china. What are the differences between a casual stoneware and a formal fine china? The weight is the most obvious distinction. Stoneware and earthenware are thicker and heavier than fine china. As odd as it may seem, they are less durable because of this. They aren't fragile, by any means, but they are more brittle than their glasslike cousin, fine china.

EARTHENWARE

Earthenware is the simplest form of pottery, formed from clay without the addition of vitreous (glasslike) material. The shaped clay is fired and then glazed with a glass coating. Its surface is porous unless glazed. The absence of the fusible ground stone in its makeup, which requires that it be fired at a lower temperature, explains why it is relatively brittle.

STONEWARE

Stoneware is made of clay to which a fusible stone (such as sand and/or ground flint) has been added. The addition of the ground stone allows it to be fired at a higher temperature, which fuses the elements into a harder material. Stoneware, though somewhat stronger than earthenware, is still heavy and opaque.

FINE CHINA

Fine china is the most glasslike of china. This is due to the combination of kaolin clay (a particularly fine white clay originally found in China), feldspar, and flint (along with other elements known only to the individual manufacturers). These ingredients, when fired at very high temperatures, vitrify into a hard, nonporous ceramic. Its strength allows it to be made thinner, so the resultant product is lighter and can be formed into more delicate shapes. The classic test to distinguish porcelain from other china is to hold a piece to the light to see its translucence.

BONE CHINA

Bone china is a form of fine china to which bone ash has been added, promoting the fusion of the ingredients and adding a bright white color. The process was developed and used primarily in England, and, indeed, bone china is often called English china.

Selecting a Pattern

Choosing a china pattern is one of the great pleasures—and challenges—of establishing a home. It's a pleasure because there are so many lovely patterns to choose from and a challenge because you want to choose the one that suits you, the way you live, and the way you expect to live one day.

Any fine specialty or department store will offer a wide range of china patterns from which to choose. An open-stock pattern, one that is easily found and can be added to as time goes on, is the sensible choice.

Using a bridal or gift registry can be an enormous help to you and to the people who will be selecting your gifts. It enables the store to keep track of your pattern— which pieces of it you have and don't have—and to advise your friends accordingly.

Of course, many couples choose not one, but two patterns—one fine china pattern for formal entertaining and one stoneware or other informal pattern for casual use. It is a good idea, particularly when deciding on an informal pattern, to consider whether it complements any serving pieces you may already have collected.

Nowhere is it written that the china used for the first (or any) course must match the pieces used for the rest of the meal. Many people lucky enough to have a variety of china choose different coordinating patterns for the various courses. The dinner plates may be in one pattern, salad plates in another, dessert plates in a third. The only rule to follow when serving is to make sure all the dishes in each course match one another.

Careful planning must be done in order to coordinate the patterns. Attention should be given to the background color of the main dishes to coordinate subsidiary patterns. Many people think that all white china plates are the same color, but there are warm whites and cool, bright whites, and muted ones. Color is not the only consideration, for texture and design play a part, too. A classic cool white porcelain can look odd paired with a heavy, creamy white earthenware.

One of the easiest ways to coordinate different patterns is to begin with the dinner plate and work out, looking for pleasing combinations of color, texture, and pattern. Say you have a fairly plain white dinner plate with a flower in the center. The flower has red petals, green leaves, and a touch of yellow at its center. Red seems the obvious color to coordinate, so you choose white dessert plates with a red band or a simply designed border of the same general style. But you could also pick

Basic China Needs

■

Most people when starting out try to have enough china for 8 or 12 people. Fine china is usually sold in 5-piece place settings, consisting of a dinner plate, salad and dessert plate, bread-and-butter plate, cup and saucer. Also needed are soup bowls, platters, and vegetable bowls. The services for everyday use and more formal entertaining vary a little.

Everyday or Casual

dinner plate
salad/dessert/luncheon plate
*bread-and-butter plate (can also be used
　for dessert)*
cereal bowl/soup bowl
cup and saucer or mug

Formal Entertaining

*service plate (only for the most formal
　of entertaining)*
dinner plate
salad/dessert plate
bread-and-butter plate
*soup bowl—soup plate or cream soup with
　stand or both*
coffee cup and saucer
demitasse cup and saucer (optional)
*sauce bowl (same number as for the service,
　which may also be used for desserts)*

There are many other pieces that you can add to the basic settings to make a full service, including coffeepots and teapots, extra vegetable bowls and platters, salad bowls, and tureens. These days there is also an increasing number of patterns available, both casual and more formal, with coordinating oven-to-table cooking and serving pieces.

Serving Dishes

■

The following is a list of the basic items needed:

1 cream pitcher and sugar bowl
At least 2 platters (1 large, 1 small)
At least 3 vegetable bowls (covered and open)
1 gravy boat with stand
2 covered casserole dishes
1 rectangular baking dish

Glasses for All Occasions

■

A complete set of crystal includes the following:

Stemware	**Barware**
Water goblet	*Highball glass*
Red wine glass	*Lowball glass*
White wine glass	*Old-fashioned glass*
Sherry glass	*Stemmed cocktail glass*
Champagne glass	*Martini glass*
	Punch bowl and cups
	Beer mug
	Liqueur glass
	Brandy snifter

the green and use green glass salad plates. For the service plate you might choose the yellow to coordinate. You can do the same with serving bowls and platters, using one or another element of the main pattern as the coordinating element.

Serving Dishes and Equipment

One question that often arises when creating a household, or even planning a party, is which serving dishes will be needed. The answer varies greatly depending upon how you entertain, but there are a few general guidelines.

You may choose to have all your serving pieces in the same pattern, so that all bowls, platters, tureens, covered vegetable dishes, and open vegetable dishes match one another. In the same way you may choose to have all the carving knives and forks, serving spoons, sauce spoons, salad servers, and jelly spoons in the same pattern.

You may also coordinate different elements, just as you do with china settings. There is a variety of beautiful utensils and receptacles available, and there are no longer restrictions about matching anything up. In fact, it sometimes makes for a more interesting table to coordinate different or unusual serving pieces. Often it is more interesting to serve the salad from a rich-looking wooden or lustrous crystal bowl than it is to have it appear quietly in a matching salad bowl.

Choosing Crystal

Crystal or glassware is not only an essential part of a set table, but also an opportunity to add great beauty to a setting. Fine crystal, from stemware to bowls and decanters, adds an elegant sparkle to a table that is unmatched. The variety is practically endless, too, ranging from stemware and barware to candlesticks, bowls, and decanters. Although it would certainly be nice, you don't have to have the finest crystal to set a beautiful table—nor do you have to have every size and style of glass in order to entertain well. But by starting with a few basics and demonstrating a little flexibility, you can serve a variety of needs and throughout your life broaden the scope.

What are the differences between fine crystal and plain glass? Crystal refers to brilliant, clear, high-quality glass. When lead is added to the mixture of sand and other elements forming glass, the resulting crystal is even more brilliant, heavier, and also softer, which allows it to be easily cut.

All fine crystal glassware, from stemmed wineglasses to cut-crystal tumblers, requires a remarkable amount of handwork in its creation—as many as thirty people may work on each glass formed. It's not surprising, then, that fine glassware tends to be expensive. However, no glassware looks and feels as wonderful as good-quality lead crystal.

Fine crystal aside, what do you really need to set a pretty table? You can use one all-purpose wineglass for almost all drinks. The basic size is the red wine or claret glass, which is larger than a white wineglass but smaller than a burgundy glass. Almost anything can be served in them, including morning juice, afternoon soft drinks, and evening cocktails—not to mention wine.

There is a problem, however, with using one glass for everything: you have to have a great number of these glasses. A better method is to start with the three basic sizes of stemware: the water goblet (which can serve as an iced tea and soft drink glass); the all-purpose wineglass; and a champagne glass. The champagne glass, either flute-shaped (which holds bubbles well) or the traditional coupe size (which can hold desserts and ices), is less likely to be used as much as the other two, so it's optional.

Chances are good that before you sit down to dinner you'll need so-called barware, or casual crystal glassware. The sizes you really need are a tall glass, usually known as a highball glass, which is used for all tall drinks, including mixed cocktails, soft drinks, iced tea, and milk; and a lowball glass, which is used for short straight cocktails and all short drinks, such as morning juice. Tall glasses hold about twelve ounces and short ones six to eight.

People often choose one pattern for stemware and another for barware. Since they are practically never on the table at the same time, you can coordinate them or not as you like.

Simplicity aside, suppose you are getting married and want to register for a crystal pattern or two. How many and what do you need? To form a basic service it makes sense to ask for three-piece suites of stemware to include a water goblet, red wine, and champagne or white wine glass. For barware, ask for tall glasses and short glasses. After that, there's almost no limit. Aim for at least a dozen of each basic stemmed glass and eight to a dozen of each basic bar glass, and once again order an open-stock pattern that can be added to easily since glassware does break.

Tips on Buying China, Crystal, and Flatware

■

1. *Choose open-stock patterns that you like and that can be added to easily over the years.*
2. *When choosing china, look for good-quality patterns that show crisp and even detail.*
3. *Plan on at least eight settings of casual china and twelve of formal china. A standard five-piece place setting consists of a dinner plate, salad and dessert plate, bread-and-butter plate, cup and saucer.*
4. *High-quality crystal is often demonstrated by the presence of a high lead content. Good-quality crystal should be brilliant and clear.*
5. *Plan on at least a dozen of each basic crystal stem glass and eight of each basic bar glass. The easiest method when registering is to choose three-piece suites of water goblet, red wine, and champagne or white wine glasses. Ask for both highball and lowball barware.*
6. *When choosing flatware, look for pleasing patterns that appeal to the eye—and that feel good in the hand. Pieces should have good weight, balance when held in the palm, and be easy to maneuver.*
7. *Plan on place settings to serve twelve—you can add to it as you go along. Standard five-piece place settings consist of a salad and dessert fork, dinner fork, dinner knife, soup or dessert spoon, teaspoon.*
8. *Use your china, crystal, and silver regularly—they are to be enjoyed.*

Selecting Flatware

European and American culture seemed to reach the peak of silverware "civilization" during the Victorian and Edwardian eras. Then the proper dinner table setting consisted of no fewer than fourteen pieces of silver (not all at the same time, of course). These days, whether you entertain lavishly or simply, the requirements are far fewer.

The most elegant, useful, and expensive kind of flatware is sterling silver. Sterling dresses up and down, never wears out, and comes in patterns both traditional and modern. It is an investment that will last your whole lifetime and that of your children and grandchildren. These days many people consider it a luxury that is beyond them —and there is no getting around it, it can be expensive. But there is also no substitute for it in any but the most informal entertaining. And, like china, you can choose a pattern and add pieces as you can afford them.

Although sterling is a long-term investment, there are many beautiful stainless-steel patterns available, from copies of sterling, to sleek modern designs and colorfully

Storing a silver service in tarnish-resistant flannel makes it easier to keep shining clean.

enameled casual patterns that make gorgeous table settings. The advantage of stainless steel is that, since it is usually considerably less expensive than silver, you can buy new patterns when you feel like a change without having to float a bank loan.

One way to have some fun is to serve different courses using different flatware. For instance, sets of beautiful Victorian fish knives and forks, often found inexpensively, are a great way to serve a fish dish. Fanciful dessert spoons, fruit spoons, and fruit knives also add a special touch. The only rule that you should be aware of is that each individual course must be served in the same pattern. If you do otherwise, the table will look disorganized.

Whatever kind of flatware you choose, whether it's sterling or stainless steel, look for good quality. One way to determine this is by the weight and balance of the pieces. A good heavy piece is more sturdy than a light one. Pick up each implement to see how it feels. Is it easy to use, does it fit your hand, does it balance? Since silver is used every day, like china, its feel and look are important.

Caring for China, Crystal, Silver, and Linen

Knowing how to set a beautiful table and give a party is a great joy; it's made easier, however, by keeping the equipment in good shape. When the china is clean and properly stored, the crystal sparkling, the silver polished, and the linens washed and ironed, we can entertain easily whenever we want.

There are no secrets to maintaining china, glass, silver, and linens, nor is it difficult or time-consuming. Like most things, it is much easier to keep things up now than ever before—it's all in the washing and storing. The simple checklists that follow say it all.

China

WASHING
1. When preparing to wash by hand, use a rubber mat to cushion the bottom of the sink.
2. When washing by hand, use mild soap or detergent to wash dishes and glassware.
3. Soak dishes with dried-on food in warm sudsy water and avoid using abrasives, especially scouring powders and steel wools.
4. Wash all antique china by hand. Modern china may be washed in a dishwasher.

Filling Your Flatware Needs

■

Basic Pieces

Dinner or meat fork
Dinner or meat knife
Salad, dessert, or luncheon fork
Dessert or soup spoon
Teaspoon

Extra Pieces for More Elaborate Entertaining

Butter knife
Salad or luncheon knife
Fish fork
Fish knife
Oyster fork
Demitasse spoon
Iced tea spoon

For the Table

Butter knife for informal entertaining
Serving spoons
Serving forks
Gravy or sauce ladle

Going Wild: The Complete Setting

■

Oyster fork	*Fruit spoon*
Snail fork	*Dessert spoon*
Fish fork	*Ice cream spoon*
Luncheon fork	*Teaspoon*
Dinner fork	*Demitasse spoon*
Salad fork	*Fish knife*
Dessert fork	*Steak knife*
Pastry fork	*Luncheon knife*
Cream soup spoon	*Butter knife*
Bouillon soup spoon	*Dinner knife*
Sauce spoon	*Cheese knife*
Iced tea spoon	*Fruit knife*
Tablespoon	

When choosing flatware, remember that silver lasts from generation to generation. It's a long-term investment that goes with any style of entertaining and that will probably outlast passing trends.

5. When using a dishwasher, load it properly. Place dishes securely and independent of one another so that they won't tap or rub during the cycle.
6. Use a mild dishwasher detergent.

STORING

1. Allow china to cool to room temperature before unloading from dishwasher.
2. Use plate racks to stand plates up or place a piece of flannel or paper towel between each plate when stacking.
3. Hang cups separately on a rack or stack no more than two high.
4. Allow enough room on shelves to keep china from crowding.

Crystal

WASHING

1. Fine crystal may be washed occasionally in a dishwasher, but if used regularly should be washed by hand.
2. Use a rubber mat to cushion the bottom of the sink.
3. When washing fine crystal by hand, use warm water and mild detergent. To maintain the sparkle, use ammonia in the wash water.
4. To keep crystal brilliant and spot-free, add a little vinegar to the rinse water.
5. When using a dishwasher, load it properly. Place glassware securely and independent of one another so the pieces won't tap or rub during the cycle.

STORING

1. Allow crystal to cool to room temperature before drying and polishing.
2. Store crystal right side up, to protect the delicate rims, or hang upside down on a bar rack.
3. Allow enough room on the shelves to keep crystal from crowding.

Silverware

WASHING

1. Sterling, silver plate, and stainless steel may all be washed in the dishwasher. Keep the silver and stainless separate from one another in the silverware basket.
2. Load the dishwasher with the handles of the forks and spoons pointing down and the knife handles up.
3. Use a mild dishwasher detergent.
4. Allow silver to reach room temperature before drying and storing.

Well-washed crystal gleams and sparkles.
CRYSTAL: *Tartan*

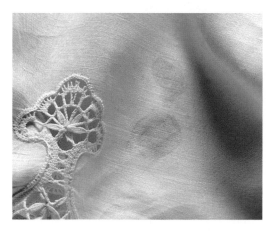

Spilling red wine on a linen tablecloth seems almost inevitable, but it's not a disaster. Just rub in salt and pour on club soda or water to neutralize the stain. Another trick some people use is to pour white wine over the red. A good soak usually helps, too.

The intricacy of old-fashioned cutwork linens can evoke an earlier era of gracious living.

5. Briefly soak the tines, bowls, and blades of silverware that have dried-on food in warm sudsy water before washing. Avoid soaking the handles of knives.

POLISHING AND STORING

1. The best way to keep silver from tarnishing is to use it regularly, so that it doesn't have a chance to darken.
2. Polish silver with a soft cloth, using mild polish.
3. Store silver in tarnish-preventive flannel in a wooden chest.

Linen

WASHING

1. Launder linens promptly after use.
2. To remove red wine stains, cover the stain with salt, rub it in, and then follow with water. Another method is to flush the stain with water and then neutralize it with a little white wine. With either method, soak the article overnight if needed before laundering.
3. To remove tomato-based stains, make a paste of laundry detergent and rub into the stain. Soak overnight before laundering.
4. Launder formal linens professionally—it's too difficult to do it well at home.
5. Informal linens may be washed and ironed easily at home.

STORING

1. Formal tablecloths may be stored neatly folded or rolled on a tube, which eliminates creases.
2. Store all linens in a dry place.

CREDITS

Matthew Klein, photographer
Linda Cheverton, stylist
Anne Disrude, food stylist

Lenox, Incorporated, thanks Alice Kolator, public relations
    director, Virginia Jackson and Celanese House and
    gratefully acknowledges:

Tables and chairs provided by Pierre Deux, New York
Linens provided by Frette
Antique picture frames and desk accessories provided by
    James II Galleries
Silver provided by Buccellati
Silver on buffet (page 71) provided by Thaxton
Flowers provided by Very Special Flowers
Wedding gown (page 28) provided by Priscilla of Boston

Index

acquaintances, 4, 6, 9, 10
active parties, 35
afternoon receptions, 52–53
afternoon tea, see tea
age groups, entertaining, 11
alcohol, 22
ambassador, title of, 107, 108
anniversary(ies), 12, 49–56
    gifts, 54–56
    parties, 52–56
    romantic dinner for two, 49–51
announcements:
    engagement, 30, 31–32
    wedding, 38

babka, 78
baby showers, 12, 56–58
baby-sitters, 18
backyard picnics, 46
baked dishes, 22
balance:
    of flatware, 134, 136
    in menu planning, 21
balloons, 60
bands, 19–21, 40
bar, full, 22, 89
barbecue parties, 35, 114
    Fourth of July, 84–85
    picnics, 89
    safety rules for, 85
barware, 133, 134
baskets, 124
bathrooms, guest, 93
bed, breakfast in, 98–99
bedrooms, guest, 93

beer, 89
best man, 39
beverages, see drinks
birthday cake, 58, 60
birthday parties, 12, 20, 58–63
    children's, 58–62
    coming-of-age dinners, 62–63
    gifts for, 62
biscuits, 94
bone china, 130
boss, entertaining the, 102–105
bouquet, bridal shower, 34
bowls, 124, 133
bread, 81, 123
bread-and-butter plate, in place settings, 120,
    121, 122–123
breakfast in bed, 98–99
bridal attendants, 29, 30, 39, 44
bridal registry, 43, 132, 134
bridal showers, 12, 29, 32–35
    etiquette for, 34
    gifts for, 32, 34
bride:
    at bridal luncheon, 29
    at bridal shop, 29
    at bridal shower, 32, 34, 35
    at postwedding party, 44
    at rehearsal dinner, 29
    wedding gifts and, 42
    at wedding reception, 39, 40, 42, 44
    at wedding rehearsal dinner, 36, 38,
        39
bride's table, at wedding reception, 44
bride-to-be, at engagement party, 29, 30, 31,
    32

brioches, 98
brownies, 84
brunch, 56
buffet cloths, 114
buffet plates, 123
buffets, 30, 34, 40, 44, 46, 54, 56, 70, 85, 96,
    102
    decorations for, 123, 124
    housewarming, 89–90
    place settings for, 123–124
burgundy glasses, 134
business associates, entertaining, 4, 7, 9, 10,
    14, 102–105

Cabinet members, title of, 107, 108
cake, 32, 58, 60, 78, 84, 85, 94, 101
cake-and-punch parties, 34
calligraphy, 126
canapés, 72
candles, 125–126
caring for china, crystal, silver and linen,
    136–139
casual:
    china, 129, 130, 132, 134
    crystal glassware, 134
    place settings, 120
casual parties, 87–99
    breakfast in bed, 98–99
    dessert, 96–97
    drop-in, 90–92
    housewarming buffets, 89–90
    picnics, 87–89
    Sunday night supper, 96–98
    weekend guests, entertaining, 92–95
caterers, 18, 38, 42, 44, 90

celebrations, 27–108
    afternoon tea, see tea
    anniversary, see anniversary
    baby showers, 12, 56–58
    birthday, see birthday parties
    boss, entertaining the, 102–105
    breakfast in bed, 98–99
    bridal showers, see bridal showers
    casual, see casual parties
    children's birthday parties, 58–62
    Christmastime cocktail parties, 69–73
    coming-of-age, 19, 62–63
    Derby Day, 82–84
    dessert parties, 96–97
    dining at the White House, 105–108
    Easter dinners, 78–79
    engagement, 29, 30–32
    formal, see formal occasions
    Fourth of July barbecues, 84–85
    holiday, 65–85
    housewarming buffets, 89–90
    New Year's Day open house, 74–76
    Passover seders, 80–82
    picnics, see picnics
    postwedding, 29, 44–47
    rehearsal dinners, 36–39
    romantic dinner for two, 49–51
    Sunday night supper, 96–98
    Thanksgiving dinners, 49, 65–69
    Valentine's Day dinner, 76–77
    wedding receptions, 29, 39–44
    weddings, see wedding
    weekend guests, entertaining, 92–95
centerpieces, 40, 102, 122, 124–125
    Thanksgiving, 69

Ceramic Art Company, viii
champagne, 72
    glasses, 134, 134
chicken, 84, 94
children:
    birthday parties for, 58–62
    Easter and, 78
    games for, 60
Chiles, James B., ix
china, viii–ix, 43, 124, 125, 129–133, 136
    basic needs in, 129, 132–33
    bone, 130
    buying, 134
    caring for, 136–137
    fine, 130
    kinds of, 130–131
    Lenox, viii–ix
    patterns, 129, 132–133
    in place settings, 116
    serving dishes and equipment, 133
Christmastime cocktail parties, 69–73
Christmas tree and ornaments, 70
claret glasses, 134
clearing plates, 105, 122
clothing, baby, 58
cloth napkins, 88, 89
clowns, 20
coat taking, 6, 26, 104, 106
cocktail parties, 19, 34, 35, 46, 54, 101
    Christmastime, 69–73
    as engagement parties, 30
coffee, 56, 94, 96, 98, 105, 122, 123
coffee trays, 102
coleslaw, 84
coming-of-age parties, 19, 62–63
condiments, 105
Congress, U.S., ix
conversations:
    directing or redirecting, 6–7
    at White House dinners, 107, 108
cookies, 84, 101
corn on the cob, 84, 85
cornucopia arrangements, 124
corsages, bridal shower, 32
coupe size glasses, 134
courses, 21
    china for, 132
    flatware for, 136
    glassware for, 134
    place settings and, 120–121
cozy dinners, 30
cranberries, 65
creases, in folded linens, 114

crystal, ix, 43, 133–134, 136
    bowls, 124
    buying, 134
    caring for, 137
    flowers and fruit, 125
    glass vs., 133–134
    Lenox, ix
cucumber sandwiches, 102
cutlery, 116

decanters, 133
decorations, 124–127
    for anniversary parties, 54
    for baby showers, 56
    for buffets, 123
    for children's birthday parties, 60
    for Christmastime cocktail parties, 70
    for formal place settings, 122
    for Fourth of July barbecue, 85
    for Thanksgiving dinner, 69
    for Valentine's Day dinner, 76
Derby Day celebrations, 82–84
dessert, xi, 22, 54, 56, 94, 105, 122, 123
    parties, 96–97
    plates, 122, 132
    service, 121, 122, 123
dinner(s), 34, 35, 54
    groom's, 39
    plates, 122, 123, 132
    informal, place settings for, 120–122
disasters, 7
disc jockeys, 20
dish towels, 114
Draper, Dorothy, 3
dressing, 6, 104
    for Derby Day celebrations, 82
    for dinner, xi
    for White House dinner, 106
dressing the table, *see* setting the table
drinks, 6, 26, 46, 72, 82, 84, 89–90, 92, 104, 134

earthenware, 130
Easter baskets, 78
Easter dinner, 78–79
Easter eggs, coloring, 78
eggnog, 72
eggs, 94, 98, 81
    Easter, 78
    stone, 124–125
engagement announcement, 30, 31–32
engagement parties, 29, 30–32
English China, 130
entertaining, art of, 1–26

entertainment:
    at children's parties, 60
    on New Year's Day, 75, 76
    organizing, 19
    at White House dinner, 108
entrees, xi, 123
equipment:
    for picnics, 88, 89
    renting, 17–19, 72, 90
everyday china, 129, 130, 132

family:
    anniversary parties given by, 52
    at engagement party, 30
    entertaining, 4
    at postwedding party, 46
    seating arrangements and, 113
    at Thanksgiving dinner, 67
    at wedding reception, 40, 42
    at wedding rehearsal dinner, 36
figurines, 124
final think-through, 26
final touches, 126–127
fine china, 129, 130, 132
finger bowls, 108, 122
finger foods, 72
first course(s), xi, 104–105, 121–122, 123, 132
    plate or bowl, 122
First Lady, 106, 107, 108
fish, 84, 94
flan, 94
flatware, 135–136
    buying, 134
    lists of, 136
    patterns, 135–136
    in place settings, 116
flower girls, 44
flowers, 40, 42, 46, 69, 78, 85, 90, 94, 96, 102, 122, 123, 124, 125, 127
    artificial, 125
    dried, 126
flute-shaped glasses, 134
folding napkins, 115, 126
food:
    for Christmastime cocktail party, 72
    for Fourth of July barbecue, 84
    at picnics, 88
    preparing, 24–26
formal occasions, 12, 21, 46, 101–108, 114, 126
    afternoon tea, *see* tea
    boss, entertaining the, 102–105
    candles for, 125
    china for, 129, 130, 132, 134

dining at the White House, 105–108
    invitations for, 14–16
    napkins for, 115
    place settings for, 108, 122–123
    social dinners, 106
Fourth of July barbecue, 84–85
French toast, 94
friends:
    baby showers given by, 56
    bridal showers given by, 32, 35
    at engagement party, 29, 30
    entertaining, xi, 3, 4, 9, 10–11
    at Thanksgiving dinner, 67
    at wedding reception, 40
fruit, 94, 127

games:
    bridal shower, 32–33
    children's, 60
    Derby Day, 82–83
garden parties, 34
gifts:
    anniversary, traditional, 54
    baby shower, 56, 58
    birthday, 62
    bridal registry and, 43, 132, 134
    bridal shower, 32, 34
    bride and groom, 39
    china as, 129
    coming-of-age, 122
    party favors as, 126
    wedding, 42
    wedding attendant, 39
glassware, 116, 133–134, 136
    barware, 133, 134
    crystal, *see* crystal
    in place settings, 116, 120
    stemware, 133, 134
glogg, 72
Glorious Food Caterers, 22
groom:
    at bridal shower, 29, 32, 34, 35
    at postwedding party, 44
    at rehearsal dinner, 29
    wedding gifts and, 42
    at wedding reception, 39, 44
    at wedding rehearsal dinner, 36, 38, 39
groomsmen's gifts, 39
groom-to-be, at engagement party, 29, 30, 32
guest lists, 10–11
    bridal shower, 35
    for housewarming buffets, 90
    seating arrangements and, 112
    for weddings, 38

guest of honor, 108
    man, 107
    woman, 104, 105, 107
guests, 7, 24
    at birthday parties, 62
    at bridal shower, 34
    inviting, *see* invitations
    at wedding rehearsal dinner, 36
    weekend, 92–95
    White House, invitations to, 107

ham, 78
hamburgers, 84
handwriting, 126
help, hiring, 17–19, 72, 105
highball glasses, 134
holiday parties, 20, 65–85
    Christmastime cocktail, 69–73
    Derby Day, 82–84
    Easter dinner, 78–79
    Fourth of July barbecue, 84–85
    New Year's Day open house, 74–76
    Passover seder, 80–82
    Thanksgiving dinner, 65–69
    Valentine's Day dinner, 49, 76–77
hors d'oeuvres, 40, 46, 54
hostesses, hosts, 3–7, 10, 92, 93
    children as, 60–61
    disasters and, 7
    five basic rules for, 7
    key qualities of, 6
    party favors from, 126
    seating arranged by, 36, 112–113
    welcoming guests as, 4–6, 24
hot dogs, 84
housecleaners, 18
house preparation, 6, 104
housewarming buffets, 89–90

ice cream, 94
Idone, Christopher, 22–24
Independence Day, 84
informal dinners, 21, 114–115
    place settings for, 120–122
introductions, 6, 104, 105
    at White House, 107
invitations, 12–16
    bridal shower, 34, 35
    formal, 14–16, 106
    for housewarming buffet, 90
    to tea, 13
    telephone, 12, 92
    wedding, 38
    to the White House, 106
    written, 12–14

Jenkins, Nancy Harmon, 7
juice, 98

Kentucky Derby, 82

lace:
    place mats, 114
    tablecloths, 113
lamb, 78, 81
Lanin, Lester, 19
Lenox, Walter Scott, viii
Lenox china, viii–ix
Lenox crystal, ix
lighting, 125–126
linen, 43, 113, 114, 124, 125, 136
    caring for, 139
    napkins, 115
    place mats, 114
liqueurs, 105
listeners, in seating arrangements,
    113
lists, in planning, 24–26
lowball glasses, 134
luncheon, 21
    for bridal attendants, 29, 39
    cloths, 114
    napkins, 115
    place mats, 114

maid of honor, 34, 39
main courses, 105
matching dishes and utensils, 132–133
matching flatware, 136
Maxwell, Elsa, 9
mayonnaise spoilage, 88
meat, 94
mementos, personalized, 52
men, in seating arrangements, 108,
    112
men's events, 29, 32, 34, 56
menus:
    afternoon tea, 101–102
    New Year's Day open house, 75
    planning, 21–24
mint juleps, 82, 84
mixers, 22
muffins, 94, 98
mulled cider and wine, 72
music, 19–21, 54

napkins, 115–116, 121–122, 123
    cloth, 88, 89
    folding, 115, 126
New Year's Day open house, 74–76
New York Times, 7

office bridal showers, 34
open house, New Year's Day, 74–76
open-stock patterns, 132, 134

pancakes, 94
parents:
    at bridal shower, 34
    at engagement party, 29, 31, 32
    postwedding party given by, 44–46
    at wedding reception, 40, 42, 44
party favors, 60, 76, 126
party games:
    bridal shower, 32–33
    children's, 60
    Derby Day, 82–83
party-giving, x–xii
    developing entertainment instincts for, x–
        xi
    organization and planning in, xi–xii
    planning for success in, 9–26
    see also hostesses, hosts
Passover seder, 80–82
pastries, 101
patterns:
    china, 129, 132, 134
    choosing, 43
    crystal, 134
    flatware, 134, 135–136
    serving dish, 133
    stemware, 134
    utensil, 133
picnic(s), 84, 87, 89, 114
    baskets, 87–88
    cloths, 88, 89
pies, 94
piñata, 58–59
pissaladière, 72
place cards, 9, 78, 107–108, 121, 122,
    126
place mats, 98, 113, 114–115
place settings:
    for buffets, 123–124
    casual, 120
    choosing, 116–124
    formal, 108, 122–123
    goal of, 116–117
    informal dinner, 120–122
    menus at, 126
planning parties, 9–26
    food preparation in, 24–26
    guest lists in, *see* guest lists
    hiring help, 17–19, 72, 105
    at home or other places, 16–17
    invitations in, *see* invitations
    menu planning in, 21–24

organizing entertainment, 19–21
    renting equipment, 17–19, 72, 90
plates:
    in buffets, 123–124
    clearing, 105, 122
    in place settings, 120
platters, 133
polishing silverware, 139
political views, seating arrangements and, 113
pool parties, 34, 92
postwedding parties, 29, 44–47
potatoes, 78
potato salad, 84
potluck, 72
    dessert party, 96
    at Thanksgiving dinner, 67–68
President of the United States, 106, 107, 108
protocol, 106
pumpkin pie, 65
punch, 58

quiet parties, 35

Reagan, Ronald, viii
receiving line, 42
    forming, 44
    at White House dinner, 106–107
receptions, 19
red wine glasses, 134
rehearsal dinners, 36–39
renting equipment, 17–19, 72, 90
Representatives, title of, 107
response, to invitations, 15–16
    written, 15, 106
retiring rule, at formal occasions, 108
ribbons, 126
roasts, 22
romantic dinners, 30
    for two, 49–51
romantic parties, 76
Roosevelt, Franklin D., viii
runners, 113, 114

salad, xi, 22, 84, 105
    casual place settings and, 120
    dressings, 22
    in formal place settings, 123
    plates, 122, 123, 132, 133
sandwiches, 101–102
savings bonds, 58
seating arrangements, 36, 69, 104, 126
    organizing, 111–113
Secret Service, 106
seder, Passover, 80–82
service plates, 121, 122, 123, 126, 133

serving bowls, 133
serving dishes, china, 133
setting the table, 94, 98, 102, 111–127
    choosing place settings in, 116–124
    decorations in, *see* decorations
    dressing the table, 113–116
    final touches in, 126–127
    lighting in, 125–126
    napkins in, 115–116
    organizing seating arrangements in, 111–113
    place cards in, 126
    place mats in, 114–115
    tablecloths in, 113–114
shy people, 6
silverware, 43, 135–136
    in buffets, 123
    caring for, 137–139
    in place settings, 116, 120
"sixteen" parties, 62
soups, 22
special needs, menu and, 68
spontaneous entertaining, 90–92
spouses, at baby showers, 56
stainless steel flatware, 135–136, 137–139
    in place settings, 116, 120
State Department, U.S., ix
stemware, 133, 134
sterling silver, *see* silverware
stews, 22
stone eggs, 124–125
stoneware, 129, 130
storing:
    china, 137
    crystal, 137
    linen, 139
    silverware, 139

streamers, 126
stuffing, 65
Sunday lunches, 34
Sunday night supper, 96–98
Supreme Court justices, title of, 107
surprise parties, 12
    anniversary, 52
    bridal showers, 35
sweet potatoes, 65

table blankets, 114
tablecloths, 98, 113–114
tablecraft, techniques of, 109–139
    caring for china, crystal, silver and linen, 136–139
    china, *see* china
    choosing place settings in, 116–124
    crystal, *see* crystal
    decorating the table, *see* decorations
    seating arrangements and, 111–113
    selecting flatware, 135–136
    setting the table, *see* setting the table
table pads, 114
tableware, 129–139
    see also specific items
tailgate picnics, 88–89
talkers, in seating arrangements, 113
tall glasses, 134
tapers, 125
tastes, guests', 24
tea, 19, 34, 96, 98, 101–102
    invitation to, 13
    proper pot of, 102
    for spontaneous entertaining, 92
    weekend, 70
tea service, 102
telegrams, singing, 32

telephone, inviting by, 12, 92
Thanksgiving dinner, 65–69
theme parties, 60, 127
three-course meals, xi
timing, in menu planning, 22, 26
    Thanksgiving dinner, 67
titles, of prominent officials, 107
toasts:
    at coming-of-age dinners, 62
    at wedding reception, 40
    at wedding rehearsal dinners, 38
trays:
    breakfast, 98
    coffee, 102
    tea, 102
Truman, Harry S., viii
tureens, 124
turkey, Thanksgiving, 65
    tending to, 68
"twenty-one" parties, 62

Valentine's Day dinners, 49, 76–77
vegetables, 22, 94, 123, 124
vice-president of the United States, ix
videotapes:
    of children's movies or cartoons, 60
    homemade, 55–56
votive candles, 125
vows, renewing, 52

waiters, 90
washing:
    china, 136–137
    crystal, 137
    linen, 139
    silverware, 137–139

water goblets, 134
watermelon, 84
wedding(s), 12, 14, 29–47
    cake, 40, 54
    engagement parties, 29, 30–32
    gifts, 42
    invitations, 38
    parties after, 29, 44–47
    receptions, 29, 39–44
    rehearsal dinners, 29, 36–39
    settings for, 17
wedding attendants, 44
    gifts for, 39
    at wedding rehearsal dinner, 36, 39
weekend:
    brunch, 56
    guests, entertaining, 92–95
    tea, 70
weight, of flatwear, 134, 136
welcoming guests, 4–6
    at casual drop-in parties, 92
    weekend, 93
White House, viii, ix
    dining at, 105–108
white wineglasses, 134
wildflowers, 42
Wilson, Woodrow, viii
wine, 81, 89, 96
wineglasses, 134
women, in seating arrangements, 108, 112
women's events, 29, 32, 34, 56
written invitations, 12–14

Yellow Pages, 19, 20